A SHEARWATER BOOK

Epicurean Simplicity

EPICUREAN
SIMPLICITY

STEPHANIE MILLS

Drypoint engravings by Glenn Wolff

Island Press / SHEARWATER BOOKS
Washington • Covelo • London

A Shearwater Book
Published by Island Press

Library of Congress Cataloging-in-Publication Data
Mills, Stephanie.
Epicurean simplicity / by Stephanie Mills.
p.   cm.
Includes bibliographical references (p.   ).
ISBN 1-55963-689-0 (cloth : alk. paper)
1. Natural history—Middle West. 2. Country life—Middle West.
3. Simplicity. 4. Conduct of life. 5. Mills, Stephanie. I. Title.
QH104.5.M47 M56 2002
508.77—dc21   2001008509

British Cataloguing-in-Publication-Data available.

Printed on recycled, acid-free paper ♲
Manufactured in the United States of America
02 03 04 05 06 07 08 09 8 7 6 5 4 3 2 1

To Hunter and Hildegarde Hannum

Contents

Prelude xi

1 The Journey and the Destination 1

2 Epicurean Simplicity 19

3 Spring 41

4 The Others 63

5 Summer 87

6 Conviviality 107

7 Vocation 127

8 Autumn 147

9 Winter 169

10 Our Common Fate 189

Acknowledgments 207

Index 211

Prelude

The air seems to be vital tissue this morning, entirely alive with mayflies and countless other insects darting or arising in the sunlight, with airborne cherry petals marking the direction of the breeze and of gravity. The chirping of crickets merges into a soft, ubiquitous jingle. The spring air is their sounding board; the whole county is their guitar. Then there's birdsong, certain presences announcing themselves. Four and twenty blackbirds are chucking and clucking. Jays are dipping low through the pine branches. A mourning dove is cooing. A starling is giving its raffish wolf whistle. Some goldfinches, among them a male with an unusual black eye mask, drop by to investigate the hummingbird feeder. The sky is washed in blue. The breezes are sweet, moist, and cool. What more do I need to know of heaven? Life is the absolute. Today the whole of existence feels like a gift.

Epicurean Simplicity

1

THE JOURNEY
AND
THE DESTINATION

In this book, I relate the pleasures, as well as the virtues and difficulties, of a perhaps simpler than average North American life.

Like Henry David Thoreau, I should not talk so much about myself if there were anybody else I knew as well. Also like Thoreau, I believe that a [wo]man is rich in proportion to the number of things [s]he can afford to let alone. Some needs are absolute. Along with every other human being, I need a minimum of 2,000 calories a day, about half a gallon of water fit to drink, a sanitary means for disposing of my bodily wastes, a way to keep reasonably clean, something muscular to do for at least some part of the day, and a warm, dry place to sleep. To that biological minimum I would add intercourse with more-than-human nature and the means to a life of the mind. Meeting those needs as sparingly as possible makes abundant the kind of riches that can't be owned.

The pleasures and riches of simplicity, it seems to me, arrive mainly through the senses, through savoring the world of a given moment. Hence my invocation of Epicureanism, a Hellenic "be what thou art" philosophy premised on the trust-worthiness of the senses. It was a philosophy that extolled sim-plicity and prudence, and it had its detractors. Because Epicu-rus, the school's founder, did say, "I am unable to form any conception of the good from which has been eliminated the pleasures of eating and drinking, the pleasures of sexual love, the pleasures of music and eloquence, and the pleasures of shape and pleasant movements," the philosophy scandalized both the church fathers and the rabbinate of the first few cen-turies C.E. The fact that *epicurean* has become synonymous with *gourmet*, or even *gourmand*, is partly the result of early clerical objections to the principle that pleasure could lead to the good. From the third century C.E. onward, *Epicurean* translated as "loose liver." To refute that canard and reclaim Epicureanism are among the aims of this work.

Most of the pleasures I experience and describe are the pleasures of twenty-first-century country life. This is not farm life, or self-reliant backwoods life, but a writer's life enriched by the kind of mid-range natural history encountered on a patch of "waste" land in the upper Midwest, the region that includes Michigan, Minnesota, and Wisconsin.

My surroundings aren't pristine, but they're not currently required to produce anything or to be anything but self-willed—that is to say, wild. I get to see, hear, touch, taste, and feel a lot of nature in my days, which is good, because nature is what I care about the most. My attention to the subject of simplicity stems from that primary concern, for materialism, especially consumerism, the twentieth-century version of that doctrine, is immensely destructive of the health and beauty of what I'm calling nature. One also could call this elemental fact and presence the planetary ecosystem, biodiversity, the earth's ecology, evolution incarnate, or the wild. It's the gorgeous, intricate, staggering, mysterious, inventive, self-sustaining, dynamic, diverse, ever-evolving, entirely interdependent sodality of creatures and habitats that for billions of years now has clothed this planet in a tissue of lives—millions in kinds and billions in numbers. Being situated so as to behold a fractal bit of that is, for me, the source of vast real-world delight.

A source of bad conscience, however, is the knowledge that my way of life, austere though it may appear to the richer folk, is still ruinously exploitive of nature—not in my backyard, where I practice harmlessness toward even the wasps, but in the atmosphere, where my fossil fuel combustion's carbon dioxide is helping change the climate; in all those mountainous places where the metals and minerals that structure and drive my American life are torn from the earth; and in the flesh of fish and birds, mammals, and reptiles, where the chemicals that made the paper and plastic I use bioaccumulate, deforming reproduction.

That guilty knowledge is another argument for material simplicity. The less I consume, the less harm I do to that which I love. In a consumer society, harmless living may be simple, but it is not easy. I make no claim to exemplary harmlessness or simplicity. I wish only to share and reflect on some of my experiences of imperfectly simple living.

For my purposes, it would be handy if Epicurus had been more quotable on the subject of nature. But as a third century B.C.E. Athenian, an urbanite, he had a concept of nature quite different from mine. To Epicurus, nature comprised the universe; to me, it's most wondrous in its minute particulars.

Next to the birds and the bees, I care most about the humane. Consumerism is as destructive of our humanity as it is of nature, and Epicurean simplicity, respectful of the soul, is relevant here. Just as nature enchants me, so do art and literature; history and philosophy engross me, and at a smaller cost to the planet than, say, an inaugural ball. The humanities supply some evidence of intelligent life on the planet, sources of beauty and meaning, of truth and instruction, of inspiration and community.

There was a medieval saying that city air makes one free. In a city, no one's looking. Or they may be looking, but there are so many persons to see that censure is overwhelmed; in cities, tolerance is as necessary as breathing. Some years ago, I made my first trip to New York City since I had become rusticated. On the sidewalks, downtown and in SoHo, each face in the torrent of humanity was definite. Everybody looks like Somebody in New York. Cream rises to the cities, even if it's the cream of the grifters. Painted cakes may not satisfy hunger, but they are appetizing. Ambitious, energetic, tough people go to cities to scale the pinnacles, or to launch a lusher life than they could possibly know back in Bangladesh, Haiti, Hungary, or North Dakota.

Flying homeward from John F. Kennedy International Airport, I disembarked in Detroit to catch a flight on a regional airline. There, the flavor of humanity changed from Manhattan salmagundi to heartland soft-serve. The travelers choking the airport looked pasty, pudgy, and pragmatic. Confronting such committed blandness, I rued, and not for the first time, my decision to dwell in the upper Midwest. This bout of culture shock and invidious comparison passed, however. Before driving home, I stopped at the all-night supermarket in Boardman City to pick up a few things. Warming to the faces of the other shoppers and the store staff, I regained my appreciation for the people here, remembering that the pleasant girl checking out my groceries, the saucy Latina who had done the same in the low-ceilinged, jam-packed *supermercado* on Amsterdam Avenue, and I are not so very different. We're just trying to make the most of our lives in our own circumstances.

Still, I know I'm not the only North American who loves the continent but not its culture. On several brief visits to Europe and during a few weeks' travel in India, I've observed that my countrymen and I often think and act like babies. Euro-Americans' history is shallow, our culture experimental and profligate. In our refusal to defer gratification or practice austerity, we seem infantile as a people. Yet the seasoned Old World, alas, appears to have been gnawed to the bone and completely domesticated. Coming home to the United States, then, I return to a vast land that still harbors wildness, to a rogue state heedless in its consumption of water, soil, fossil fuel, and fat. I return to the ease of the mother tongue and the intimacy of long-standing friendships. The mental souvenirs I've dragged home from abroad reinforce my alienation. It's partly just the Goldilocks syndrome: One place lacks inland seas, another historical consciousness, and none is just right. Of course, many of us writers are temperamentally at odds with the world. It's not work one can do with a crowd.

The avalanche of blossoms on the abandoned apple trees that welcomes me back on a springtime drive home from the airport, and the ability to look out across open land, to smell the green freshness of the breeze, and to enjoy the taste of my own well water again, all make me feel a lot less crazy for having leapt, nearly twenty years ago, from the liberated climes of the city of San Francisco into the heartland insularity of the upper Midwest.

Those fields are open thanks to the people who stayed put, the keepers of the heartland. Those settlers and their descendants put in a century and a half of hard work, living rural lives, yoked with the land. A handful are still farming today, still trying to fulfill an earthbound ambition.

I spent my only childhood in a displaced place, Phoenix, Arizona, a city plopped on the Sonoran Desert like a Monopoly board game whose thirsty players keep sending out for more water. My family lived in one of the first suburbs in northeast Phoenix, in a $9,800 house bought in 1949, a few years after my Arizona dad and Mississippi mom got out of the service and married.

Thus, I was born into what Alan Thein Durning, in *How Much Is Enough? The Consumer Society and the Future of the Earth*, identifies as the consumer class, in which annual household income per family member is above $7,500 and which constitutes about one-fifth of the world's people. The consumer life, Durning says, "is among the world's premiere environmental problems."

As a member of this class, I have never wanted for any *thing*. There have been times when I've wanted for love and consolation, for some hint of meaning, or for surcease from physical or emotional pain. I've been broke often enough, but I've never known poverty, never performed without a net. I have wanted for greater energy, courage, compassion, and clarity, but so far I've never lacked anything material to a comfortable and healthy life.

It's an extraordinary position to be in on a planet that is home to a billion people living on less than $700 per annum, drinking unclean water, getting insufficient food, and living in shanties. Between the consumers and the destitute are 3.3 billion people—the world's middle-income class, earning between $700 and $7,500 per capita. Their lives of decent sufficiency don't compare well with the *Dallas* and *Dynasty* lifestyles pervading the world's airwaves but are a possible standard for both consumers and the poor.

While growing up in Phoenix, I had my fill of endless summer. People who see a bright side to global warming are sadly mistaken in imagining that perpetual heat would be nice. In 1965, I seized my first opportunity to escape the Sun Belt by going away to a small liberal arts college for women in Oakland, California. It was a heady time to be in college, even an out-of-the-way women's college. Being averse to crowds, not to say mobs, I mostly watched the Bay Area's revolutionary doings from afar, sitting out the marches and be-ins. Even so, I got radicalized.

During my senior year, through newspaper reading and a little organizing, I learned about ecology, specifically human overpopulation. Shocked by the magnitude and centrality of that problem, I wrote a speech on the subject and was elected class speaker. At the commencement exercises in June 1969, I declared that in light of overpopulation and impending ecological catastrophe, "the most humane thing for me to do would be to have no children at all."

At the time, it was shocking for a young woman to be so unilaterally drastic about motherhood, but the choice has served me well. As a feminist, I assumed that I should determine the purposes my body would serve, and I must have intuited that for me, the writer's life would be incompatible with parenthood. My renunciation was, in fact, epicurean, and it has abetted my simplicity.

Along with numerous other youthful hothead graduation speakers that June, I made national news. The resulting swirl of notoriety launched my career as an ecological wordsmith.

Many years ago, a colleague told me that I lead a charmed life. At the risk of jinxing my luck, I have to agree. It may be that the charm of my life is as simple as "Them that's got shall get." I got generous, intelligent parents who read and wrote and spoke interestingly. I got a calling. I took a principled stand a bit precociously and quite propitiously. For the next fifteen years, I remained in the San Francisco Bay Area, lecturing, writing and editing, and organizing conferences for several ecology-minded organizations and periodicals.

In 1984, I relocated from a snug but ever-pricier Telegraph Hill apartment with an East Bay view to a haphazardly renovated octogenarian farmhouse near Tamarack City. The proximate cause of my move to this lovely surround was a guy named Phil whom I'd met that spring at the First North American Bioregional Congress. Phil was a bioregional organizer, co-op activist, and hippie carpenter. Like a lot of North Woods counterculturalists, he still upheld the values of material simplicity, respect for ecology, and community despite the fact that it was the 1980s. What's more, he had a very attractive body politic. Like the fruit on the maverick apple trees around this countryside, Phil was ruddy, tangy, and free. He lived with his good friend Rob in the aforementioned farmhouse, known locally as the Hovel, as had a kaleidoscopic array of interesting hippie bachelors over the previous few years. Not long after Phil and I met and fell madly in love, I visited him for a long Fourth of July weekend. Smitten by both the man and his home, when the hint was dropped that I might come and abide awhile, I could hardly wait to move in.

That I was, on the basis of a brief encounter, two months' correspondence, and a casual invitation, going to an obscure part of the United States known mainly for cold, in a belated move back to the land, struck my friends and family as an appalling piece of impulsiveness. It would entail some heavy dues.

It was rash indeed to have pulled up stakes and followed if not my heart, then some other major organ, to a life here in the upper Midwest. Even though a handful of interested and disinterested observers hinted that the prospects for our conjugal future were doubtful, I'd left San Francisco aiming to be wed. Hindsight tells me that marriage was something I had to get out of my system, and Phil obliged me all the way.

Four months after our storybook wedding, we were in a terrible automobile accident, a head-on collision in which Phil was almost killed and I nearly lost my right leg. After hovering for a week at death's door, Phil beat the Grim Reaper. He walked out of the intensive care unit not long thereafter and began rehabilitating himself by helping to organize the Second North American Bioregional Congress. The injury to my leg was termed the "maximum sustainable." It took about four years and six surgeries to fix it, so I went through intermittent bouts of hospitalization, pain, and disability for a while.

While Phil and I were still in the hospital, someone pointed us in the way of a plaintiffs' attorney who had just settled a civil suit against the state concerning the very stretch of highway where Phil and I had been hurt, arguing that the road was marked in a way that conduced to mayhem. We, too, sued, and three years later we each won a goodly sum of money. I like to think of mine as my Crashenheim, a state arts grant.

Meanwhile, about a year after the accident, Phil and I needed to clear out of the Hovel. Rob's wife-to-be, Peggy, and her two daughters had also taken up residence there, and we all needed more room. On the northeast corner of Rob's seventy-five acres, Phil and I set about building ourselves a house.

My participation in the construction was as much as I could manage, on and off canes and crutches, in and out of casts and braces. I gardened a little and dug a trench for the foundation. I drove a lot of nails in the subfloor. I cooked for the worker bees and tried to feed my good cook of a husband, who was bringing home the tofu and laboring on our house after he returned from his job with a small construction company. Most of the time, though, I read and wrote and thought, none of which bought any thermal-pane windows.

A trim little place of our own design, financed by a loan from my parents and raised with a great deal of help from our friends, resulted. Meanwhile, our strike-anywhere match was guttering out. On Christmas Eve in 1988, Phil and I moved into our slightly unfinished house. By Valentine's Day of 1989, we'd split up. The divorce was final that July. I bought Phil's equity, got the deed, and became a householder in my own right. Thus the horrible providence of divorce.

The five acres we'd bought from Rob had been farmed out years before and then planted with rows of Scotch pine, a Christmas tree crop. We did only a minimum of clearing for our homesite, and over the years the pines have continued to grow, along with young sugar maples, cherries, poplars, and beeches—trees native to this place that are reclaiming their territory. Even though I'm in earshot of my neighbors, it looks as though I live deep in a forest, although not one primeval.

A few years after I regained my single status, I had the opportunity to purchase another thirty acres from Rob, expanding my scruffy nature preserve considerably. A piece of paper says this land is mine—not the nuthatches', not the Scotch pines', not the red squirrels', not the knapweed's or the pin cherries', not the grasshoppers' or the blackflies'. Barring untoward changes in regime, my tenure is secure as can be. The truth of the relationship, however, is not so much a matter of my owning the place as of the place owning me.

Place is sensual. "The brain has blood in it," says archetypal psychologist James Hillman. We have eyes, ears, noses, and fingertips with which to pay attention. Also tongues, for tasting snowflakes or wild strawberries. We are nothing if not sensate beings.

The knowledge that surrounds me is awesome: how to fly, how to hover, how to find the film of water on a soil particle, how to locate a mate with only a pheromone molecule for a clue, how to grow thirty feet tall in sandy soil. My land sustains the ground of my being, grants me the privilege of belonging to a community whose every last member—from snow fleas to chickadees to lichens to serviceberries to voles to grouse to garter snakes to coyotes to white-tailed deer to white birches, basswoods, and barred owls—"knows way more than I do," as anthropologist-author Richard Nelson's Koyukon hunting mentor told him.

In one way or another, I have been dwelling in the same place, among the same countercultural friends and alongside the same real-life neighbors, for upward of fifteen years now. All the life of the place is my community, really, from the periodical cicadas buzzing on a humid late-July evening to the red squirrels yabbering year-round in the acres of pines.

Details are my delight. In the country, many of the details have minds of their own: lady beetles crowding around, seeking winter hibernacula; knapweed flourishing everywhere; a raccoon and her pudgy kits climbing a cherry tree; a crow japing overhead. All this living, self-willed detail informs me in ways that cities no longer do.

Often, on a late-night transit from my house to my writing studio, I can see the galaxies coursing overhead. My place is far enough out in the country, and the region's ambient light is low enough, that on a cloudless night I walk in starlight that's cold and bright as diamonds. To be able to see just how full the night sky can be is both a perfect wonder and, to me, a necessity.

When I left San Francisco in 1984, it was in hope of finding a partnership conducive to living simply and self-reliantly, of forging a tie with the land. It turns out that living in the country and making a living in the country are two different things. My attainments in simple living and self-reliance are middling, owing mostly to my early and public decision not to have children and to the meager income that rewards the writing life. I try to limit my damage, and being in no danger of becoming rich helps.

Most people's definition of *enough* is "just a little more," and in my first impulse I am not unlike most people. Still, because I am persuaded of that Thoreauvian precept that real wealth is a disinterest in the acquisition of things, and because I suspect that the ultimate wealth might be to be entirely freed of the need for things, I regard my advantages, privileges, and comforts also as liabilities. Conveniences quickly become necessities. They have enabled my ignorance of some fundamental survival skills and cost me opportunities in resourcefulness.

The hardihood it took to live here in the upper Midwest a century or ten centuries ago was integral. Form followed function. Hunters and trappers, then farmers and loggers and their womenfolk, probably didn't fret, as I do, about body image, but about how to produce enough food to sustain a tremendous amount of hard work, such as raising barns or families of nine children, both of which got done eighty years ago at the homestead that eventually became the Hovel. They slogged around in buffalo or bearskin robes, woolens, and leather boots, not Gore-Tex or Polarfleece clothing. Living through the typical woman's day in those circumstances no doubt would feel like a violation of my human rights and help clarify why it is that people embrace progress with such abandon.

The twentieth-century notion of progress entailed ever-increasing reliance on goods and resources brought from afar and brokered centrally. Most of my post-progress household's economy—electric service; propane for cooking; gasoline for driving; paper, metals, and food—is imported from outside the bioregion and as such is not sustainable. Long lines of supply are costly and vulnerable to disruption.

Living in the country in the modern way seems to entail using a car, or maybe the car makes it possible to live in the "woodburbs" in a non-self-reliant way. It comes down to the fact that my Toyota wagon makes a direct annual contribution to the greenhouse effect, which is changing the weather and degrading the country. So my way of life is threatening my way of life. Like so many well-intentioned people, I'm caught in a monkey trap.

As Tolstoy pointedly summed it up, "I sit on a man's back, choking him and making him carry me, and yet assure myself and others that I am very sorry for him and wish to ease his lot by all possible means—except by getting off his back."

Finding ways to walk my talk and reduce my complicity is a long-term project. It's some consolation to know that I'm not the only aspiring simplifier who's found it difficult to unclench her tiny fists from some amenity. In "Voluntary Simplicity," a seminal article published in 1937, Richard Gregg told of fretting aloud to Mahatma Gandhi that truly to simplify, Gregg would have to give up his library. Gandhi responded: "As long as you derive inner help and comfort from anything, you should keep it. If you were to give it up in a mood of self-sacrifice, or out of a stern sense of duty, you would continue to want it back, and that unsatisfied want would make trouble for you."

Like personal mobility, my solitude isn't something I'm ready to give up. Yet I am persuaded that individualism, if not individuality, is a major obstacle to the sharing of goods that is essential to the truly simple life. Facing my own complicities, I've concluded reluctantly that the simple life is not something best practiced in isolation, at least not by a person of sub-Gandhian character.

The harmful aspect of living alone is being the sole consumer of one of everything rather than being part of a household or community in which many things may be shared. Certainly, a society reduced to its least common denominator of singletons, one to a dwelling, is the ultimate market, with each and every person a consumer wanting his or her very own hot tub, lawn mower, and espresso machine.

On the other hand, a singleton can run a frugal household without worrying about depriving anyone (like children) of a normal way of life and without nudging spouse or offspring on conservation measures like using leftover water from the cat's drinking bowl to irrigate houseplants or mandating that the dishes be washed in an aqua-frugal, if less than perfectly hygienic, way.

Some conservation and hardihood is built into my household infrastructure. Such high-minded measures can lose their luster, become onerous, but they remain commitments nonetheless. There is wood heat, for instance, to which I am structurally committed by the deliberate omission of any other economical means of heating my house. As of February 2001, midpoint of a gray, snowy winter, the corollary virtues of wood heat were long forgotten, but it remained my only good source of warmth. Somehow, I had imagined that all the work a woodstove involves would get easier the longer I did it, but every year it becomes more difficult. I forgot to factor in the aging process.

Of a chilly morning, I may be found on the couch swaddled in a spiffed-up comforter, drinking gunpowder tea. The only sounds in the house are the draft of the woodstove and the ticks and creaks of its sheet steel, of the cat giving herself a bath, and of my own digestion and the stroking of graphite on paper. A blue jay near the bird feeder might make a commotion. In such moments, I lead the perfect life, with comfort, solitude, a spacious privacy, and the invitation to write. Yet in the midst of such moments, I clutch at my comforts and necessities, fearing the day when I may have to do without if, say, the economic house of cards in whose cozy attic this wordmonger dwells is collapsed by a gust of ecological reality. "Scratch a fear, find a wish; scratch a wish, find a fear," said my friend Felicia Guest.

Troubling awareness of the growing inequality within human societies and the encroaching scarcity or contamination of the basics—food, fuel, water, shelter—is part of the reason I value my own sleek simplicity so acutely. In this world, that there is food for me when I want to eat amazes me. I can even be choosy about my midnight snack: Graham crackers or whole-wheat toast? Yogurt or banana? Soy milk or herb tea? I savor the food and choke back the thought of all the hunger on earth. Heightening that awareness is the fear that someday there might not be food for *me* to eat; then I'll go bereft of victuals, let alone choices of what to savor.

The paradox is that I seem to be having a good time on the eve of destruction. Seeing the degradation of land and life at the planetary and neighborhood scales causes me pain. Yet every day, sooner or later, some living pleasure overtakes me. It could be the midnight coyote chorus or an owl asking, "Who cooks for you, oo, oo?" It could be a letter from a friend, the preparation and enjoyment of a meal, or a walk out back to plant acorns. Love confronts death daily, and so far, it's a draw.

The place where I live now is not a summerland of eternal youth but a realm of cycling change. Each year is a parable begun in stillness and chill, of bare ground warmed with spring life returning, then bursting, buzzing, peaking in summer, and issuing a final flare in autumn, to subside in another winter's seeming nullity. The genius loci here is quadripartite, embodied in the four seasons.

Just as the earth's daily rotation and annual trip around the sun drive the whole show, they drive this narrative. This book moves through a composite year, a round of the seasons in this region. Everything I describe is actual, but some bits and pieces have been moved around for aesthetic reasons.

With all the variations in the years, time's passage is sure. Apples growing rubicund amid the summer-green foliage note that one paradisaical season is peaking to give way to another more brisk. This kind of time sense isn't calendrical. Industrial civilization's dates and months are the same; the clock reigns. Minutes and hours divide the time uniformly, whereas in the real world, days, moons, and moments are unalike—beautiful or terrible, unexceptional or tremendous.

Living near the earth in a climate with dramatic extremes presages certain difficult realities of human existence. Ineluctable changes such as the blooming and withering of wildflowers and weeds through the summer remind me that in both the short and long runs, our days are numbered.

On August 17, 1998, my mother died as she was about to dish up some soup for Dad's lunch. We had known that her lung cancer was incurable, but what carried her off was a massive heart attack. Mama's death occurred in the midst of this writing, and I was stunned by grief for a long stretch of time.

Mourning my mother's death, missing her, and trying still to understand her overpowered me. Yet it is in the nature of grief to abate, for time and the memory of love to assuage the pain of great loss. Bereavement is chokingly personal and common as midnight; I don't wish to cannibalize mine, but grief has informed many of my daily experiences. It has made quite poignant the Epicurean pleasures and existential questions with which my life is well supplied.

"Nothing lasts forever, Stephanie," said a friend, a Zen bridegroom on his wedding day, in response to my tactless wish that this third marriage of his might endure. Stars collapse upon themselves; mountains are worn down; every species eventually becomes extinct or vanishes into something different. Climate changes, empires devolve and crumble, different generations of gods know their twilight, hemlines rise and fall, the flesh wrinkles and sags, the goodies all get eaten. The impermanence of the universe is manifest, inescapable. I know that, yet I am immoderately attached to this life, these pleasures, this place.

2

EPICUREAN
SIMPLICITY

January had gone, and the sunny afternoon's weather forecast made it sound as if the conditions for skiing were fleeting. I dressed to go out, hopped on my skis, and headed west, emerging from the pines that surround the house to hurtle, screaking and sizzling, down a little hill on a thin layer of glitter dusting a half-inch crust. The snow's surface crumbled noisily under my weight, marking my tracks and breaking my speed. I tried to be cautious enough not to sprain or break any of my limbs out of ear- or eyeshot of help. Mild hazard puts an edge on the sport's savor. I crossed Rob's land and continued toward another neighbor's woodlot. Freezing fogs the night before had coated the bare trees' topmost branches and twigs with ice. The wind was disquieting the trees, sending glassy sheaths shivering down to the snow-covered ground. That fog had also lacquered pine needles; fine ice hypodermics glinted in the blue shadows at the base of the evergreens.

The difference between the temperature of my insides and that of the world outside might have been as much as 90 degrees Fahrenheit. The air drawn in through my nostrils might have been as cold as 5 or 10 degrees, but my heart's blood was suffusing my body at its usual 98.6 degrees. Inhaling, I could feel the cold sting—that startling aridity of freezing air—and in the same instant swelter in my clothing, heated from within by metabolism and from without by the sun baking my shoulders. I skied for an hour or so. Wind, snow, and sunlight put beauty everywhere I looked. After turning toward home, I glided and let the lower half of my body pilot, steering with my toes, pushing with my calves, banking with my thigh muscles, flexing my ankles and knees and hip joints. Every so often, I'd stop to raise my face skyward, listen to the silence, and let the sunshine glow redly through my closed eyelids. My heart's utterance was "Thank you. Thank you. Thank you."

Home from the ski and then fresh from a shower, I was enjoying my cleanness and the ease that follows a little exertion. The cat was promenading around my shins under the dining table, touching me. I took my evening meal by fire- and candlelight, looking out through the glass door to the still and floodlit backyard. Countless chickadee and squirrel tracks were scribbled in the snow, all paths converging at the bird feeder. But in the black-and-whiteness of this starry February night, the only creature to be seen stirring was me. My reflection, consisting mainly of the glint of my salad fork traveling briskly mouthward, bounced back from the glass.

As I savored the crumbs of blue cheese in the salad that rounded out my Sunday dinner, I was thinking of Epicurus. During his heyday in the third century B.C.E., Epicurus propounded pleasure, simplicity, and friendship as the means and ends of the good life. But, said the Roman philosopher Seneca a few centuries later, to Epicurus pleasure was something "small and slender," an absence of pain, especially that which results from excess or craving. World-renowned in his day, Epicurus wrote prolifically, but only fragments of his writings survive. Among them is an endearing request in a letter to a friend: "Send to me some Cythnian cheese," Epicurus wrote, "so that, should I choose, I may fare sumptuously."

I'd purchased most of the ingredients for my meal—beans, rice, and produce—from our local natural foods co-op. The cheese, however, I had purchased by sweat equity from the market in nearby Pineville. Whereas the co-op is fifteen automobile miles distant, the Pineville Market is a brief, scenic bike ride away. The thought of my friendly relations with its proprietor, who once upon a time was my husband, and of the fun I had painting the sign for the grocery store Phil and his wife now run, enhanced the flavor of the cheese. Furthermore, the idea that in regarding the cheese as a treat I was of a mind with a Hellenistic philosopher made a tasty side dish.

I'd been drawn to Epicurus by a shiny magpie's shard of knowledge. I associated the term *Epicurean* with a refinement of taste and an ability to savor. As I ruminated on the proposition of simple living, it seemed to me that if in our time we could learn to savor the goodness of little, everyday things, we could get more out of less and abandon our ruinous gluttony. Furthermore, in my own experiments in simple living, I hoped to relinquish my gluttony for punishment—my puritanism and apocalyptism—in favor of the sensuous. The Roman poet Lucretius, literature's foremost Epicurean, said of the senses, "These we trust, first, last, and always."

Consulting my *Encyclopaedia Britannica*, eleventh edition, the gift of a friend, I followed *Epicurean* upstream to its source and found an engaging article on Epicurus by one William Wallace. A Scot, Wallace was a professor of moral philosophy at Merton College Oxford. Had he not written of Epicurus so winningly, my interest in the old Greek might have faded. But the gift of a good teacher, which Wallace, according to his contemporaries, surely was, is to engender interest in his or her subject.

Epicurus' wisdom, wrote Wallace, "was to go back to nature and find a wider and more enduring foundation for ethical doctrine, to go back from words to realities." The Epicureans made a practice of frugality and prudence. According to some sources, they lived communally. They were united in their devotion to Epicurus and his philosophy and by their friendship. Suspecting that I might have found my patron sage, I sought to learn more.

I satisfy my curiosity in an old-fashioned way. Rather than going to the Internet, I go to the library and allow its limitations to direct my search. The Internet is too vast, the quality of what one finds there too mixed, and the search-engine logic too different from mine. Besides, I have no ambition to cope with all the information in the world. And I do love going to the library.

In pursuit of Epicurus, I went to the local community college library's compact philosophy shelf. In Whitney J. Oates' introduction to *The Stoic and Epicurean Philosophers*, I read that Epicurus was a monist, unlike Plato and his ilk, who saddled the West with its idealism. The schizoid notion that there's an ideal out yonder, of which this life is a dim and inferior version, seems to be a formula for discontentment with the real. Perhaps, like spiritual philosopher Ram Dass, a contemporary Epicurean would enjoin the truth-seeker to Be Here Now and Pay Attention.

Once one has asked the "To be or not to be" question and answered it in the life-affirmative, one's life becomes a deed.

How are we to live—not merely survive? This may be the most serious ethical question we now face. In antiquity, it was the work of philosophers to raise serious questions and to hash out the answers in their schools. Figuring out everything was the philosopher's bread and butter. A philosophy began with a construct of the essential nature of reality. Before the philosopher could propound human verities, she or he had to explain the universe. Twenty-three centuries ago, however, inquiring minds didn't build linear accelerators, electron microscopes, or telescopes to examine nature; they just cogitated hard and came up with propositions so coherent and complete that they *had* to be true. The philosopher's purview ranged from atoms to eternity and from the nature of the soul to a vision of the good society. A question like "How are we to live?" had to be considered in cosmic totality.

Epicurus went at it with philanthropic zeal. Among his aims was to free men and women from their fear of death by his argument that when life's over, it's over. There's no Hades, no rebirth, no guilt to follow beyond the grave, and no punishment thereafter. The Epicurean philosophy that what you sense is what you get, and that this life is ample, was so liberating and embraceable that generations of Greeks and Romans revered Epicurus. Perhaps his existentialism was as attractive in early times as John Lennon's "Imagine there's no heaven / It's easy if you try / No hell below us / Above us only sky / Imagine all the people / Living for today" has been in ours.

Epicurus was not terribly intellectual as Greek philosophers went. As Wallace tactfully put it, "Epicureanism with its freedom from logic and metaphysics, its direct appeal to the ordinary mind, the pathos of its ethical tone, and the humanistic character of its historical philosophy, seems more congenial to poetry than any of its contemporary systems."

Epicurus was mainly interested in everyday reality and more concerned with helping people to live in amicable contentment than with publicly debating his philosophy. (This is not to say that he couldn't hurl insults and epithets as well as his fellow sages. Philosophical disputes, usually splenetic, may have filled the niche in ancient times that professional wrestling does in ours.)

The Stoic and Epicurean Philosophers contained the extant remains of Epicurus' 300 volumes, reduced by neglect and time to a scant twenty-two pages. Contrary to Epicurus' intentions, his opus is succinct. Thus, most of what is known of Epicurus comes to us by way of his defenders, his critics, and the Roman poet Lucretius, his greatest disciple.

In *The Nature of Things,* written in the middle of the last century B.C.E., Lucretius expounds Epicurus' philosophy. Lucretius' masterpiece, cast as an argument, surely owes a measure of its vivacity to being a spirited defense of the master's achievement.

Serendipitously, a few years before embarking on this book of mine, I had acquired a copy of Frank O. Copley's translation of Lucretius' *The Nature of Things.* Knowing only that Lucretius was in the same league as Virgil and Ovid, when I chanced on the book in a used bookstore, I snapped it up. Someday, I thought, I might get around to some classical edification. Little did I suspect that there would come a day when I would find myself seduced by Lucretius' astounding poem, his stunning imagery, and laughing at his worldly wisdom.

Copley thought Epicurus had adduced his physics—the idea that the universe consists entirely of atoms and void—cursorily, as a matter of good philosophical form. Lucretius, though, threw himself wholeheartedly into the challenges of illustrating Epicurean physics and of recounting the history of humankind. He may have embarked on the writing of *The*

Nature of Things out of an evangelical fervor for Epicureanism, but it seems that he persisted, and produced a masterpiece as a mighty feat of poesy. Here is how Lucretius takes up the question of

> . . . why,
>
> though all the basic particles are in motion,
>
> their total seems to stand at total rest . . .

He answers:

> For often upon a hill the fleecy flock
>
> cropping lush lands move slowly where the grass
>
> bespangled with fresh dew calls invitation,
>
> and lambs with a bellyful frisk and tease and nudge;
>
> our distant view sees this all run together,
>
> a patch of white pinned bright on deep green hills.

Far less is known of Lucretius than of Epicurus historically. But poets are a transparent lot, and what is lacking in Lucretius' biography is compensated by the schadenfreude psychology evidenced in the following passage, in which Lucretius cuts to the quick of Epicureanism—that pleasure is the pain one *doesn't* have:

> It's sweet, when winds blow wild on open seas,
>
> to watch from land your neighbor's vast travail,
>
> not that men's miseries bring us dear delight
>
> but that to see what ills we're spared is sweet;
>
> sweet, too, to watch the cruel contest of war
>
> ranging in the field when you need share no danger.
>
> But nothing is sweeter than to dwell in peace
>
> high in the well-walled temples of the wise,
>
> whence looking down we may see other men
>
> wavering, wandering, seeking a way of life,

with wit against wit, line against noble line,
contending, striving, straining night and day,
to rise to the top of the heap, High Lord of Things.
O wretched minds of men, O poor blind hearts!
How great the perils, how dark the night of life
Where our brief hour is spent! O, not to see
that nature demands no favor but that pain
be sundered from the flesh, that in the mind
be a sense of joy, unmixed with care and fear!

Epicurus and his followers understood that reducing one's wants and needs to a minimum was the likeliest way to live the unpained life, so they lived quite simply. Bread and water were their daily fare. The school of Epicurus met in a garden. As Seneca imagined it a few centuries afterward:

> When the stranger comes to the gardens on which these words are inscribed, "Friend, here it will be well for thee to abide: Here pleasure is the highest good," he will find the keeper of that garden a kindly hospitable man, who will set before him a dish of barley porridge and water in plenty, and say, "Hast thou not been well entertained? These gardens do not whet hunger but quench it: They do not cause a greater thirst by the very drinks they afford, but soothe it by a remedy which is natural and costs nothing. In pleasure like this I have grown old."

Epicurus' garden was a place apart from the world. Within its walls, enjoying their communion alfresco, the Epicureans were quietists. One of the master's answers to the question "How are we to live?" was "Live unknown." The benefit of withdrawal from the hurly-burly of the polis was elemental: "The happiness of the Epicurean," wrote Wallace, "was a grave and solemn pleasure—a quiet, unobtrusive ease of heart."

Now, I'm no quietist, but that quiet, unobtrusive ease of heart has an undeniable appeal, and citizenship hasn't become any less vexing in the past two thousand years.

Epicurus arrived at his views in a world whose top speed was that of a galloping horse or a vessel under sail, whereas our world's speed continues its silicon acceleration, dragging our prehistoric flesh behind it. These days, the manner of our living can change in fundamental ways every year. But throughout many centuries, human living was consistent, changing only gradually. Lucretius, who had the advantage of living long before the Industrial Revolution, which commoditized or combusted every atom of matter that could yield some profit, wrote out of a handmade civilization, which had no engines yet to outrace perception.

In Epicurus and Lucretius both, there was a profound respect for nature, for the senses, and for every person's inborn perception and capability. Over the past couple of thousand years, though, in the name of such phantasms as Progress, Efficiency, and Growth, Lucretius' "Earth, sweet magic-maker" has been exploited so ruthlessly that in very many places to trust one's senses and fully perceive the horror of a clear-cut, a slum, or a strip-mined mountain would be to invite catatonia. In everyday living, our senses are outdistanced by invisible threats at the atomic, molecular, and atmospheric scales. The contemporary wish either to numb or to discount the senses is not so hard to understand.

When I, S. Mills, freelance writer dwelling in the upper Midwest at the beginning of the twenty-first century, pose the question "How are we to live?" it is like standing under the business end of a coal chute and pulling the cord. Right away, I am buried and besmirched by a hard load of industrial matter. Under these circumstances, the fundamental question ramifies into "How am I to live, given ozone depletion, chemical contamination, human overpopulation, resource exhaustion, and imminent ecosystem collapse?"

Among do-gooders, it's bad form to be a pessimist, but I can't seem to get that extinction crisis out of my mind. Or that population explosion. Or global climate change. Or the consequences of an era of trade agreements. Can't get those billionaires; those landless, homeless, jobless billions; those new diseases; that global casino of finance capitalism; the corporate capture of the media; those aging nuclear reactors; those surveillance satellites; those crowded prisons out of my mind.

These days, most of us know at some level that consumerism is complicity in all the above. Even ordinary lives in our society, let alone the lifestyles of the rich and famous, exploit and undermine cultures and bioregions near and far. However suppressed or attenuated, an awareness of doing harm must taint whatever pleasure might be had from material convenience or luxury. The corporate endeavor to efface or deflect such awareness results, popularly, in an infantile belligerence and presumption of entitlement, buttressed with some very convoluted but respectably countenanced rationales for the present global condition of extreme ecological degradation and economic injustice.

Given the degree to which even low-on-the-food-chain types like me are implicated in the wholesale wastage of the earth, the structural aspect of the answer to "How are we to live?" must be "More locally." If I have direct sensory information about their consequences, I may make more responsible choices. The epitome of the good here would be to grow or make my own basic necessities. Next best would be to barter for necessities or purchase them from a neighbor whose practices I know and respect. Next to that would be buying from a reputable, socially and ecologically conscientious purveyor; the nadir, a fast-food burger from a global chain.

By paying attention to the small things—the wholesome-ness of the daily bread, the source and state of the water, the seemliness of one's shelter, and the well-being of all the human and more-than-human lives around us—we may be led to practice simplicity and harmlessness in tangible ways, to "be the change one wishes in the world," as Gandhi taught. This is not to premise a life on renunciation, abstinence, and depri-vation but to enjoy, as did Epicurus and his followers, the free-dom in simplicity.

The champions of progress are wont to say that one can't turn back the clock. However, once I left San Francisco, I managed to stop my personal clock. Consequently, my life seems to have become something of a museum of bygone mentalities, practices, and pleasures, and I am beginning to feel like a curator. After spending the first half of my adult life trying to do my bit for the macrocosm, devoting my talents and energies toward speaking a word for nature, I find myself now addressing the microcosm of my own home and the life within.

An activist's life can yield prodigies of service and no time for self-knowledge. Just for now, I want to sit in the garden, to savor my life and my solitude, to do my work, and to be a good friend. I do wish to cultivate my serenity. Whether one lives known or unknown, roaming through life hostile or anxious won't benefit the commonality. It doesn't follow, however, that serenity alone will suffice to save this world.

One afternoon as I was sweeping my house, it occurred to me that having a philosophy really can be a help. As I rhyth-mically swept the sand and ash and hair and lint and leaf-legged wood bug carcasses into neat little accumulations for the dustpan, it also occurred to me that my willingness to be behind the times has been both a cause and an effect of philosophy. A keystone of mine is that life-forms and life places have moral standing on par with that of any human being. Therefore, these "Others" are entitled to respect and all the deference and consideration I can offer as I go about satisfying my vital needs. This is a basic tenet of deep ecology, a philosophy first articulated by the Norwegian philosopher Arne Naess. The deep questioning fundamental to deep ecology helps one to distinguish between needs and wants and to minimize those that entail getting and spending. Did the world really cry out for a self-cleaning kitty litter tray? Or for any of the thousands of labor-saving, landfill-clogging gewgaws being hawked in ever more ubiquitous commercial media, from advertisements on bathroom walls to sales pitches on voice mail systems?

Having a sweeping philosophy, being able to spend an hour tidying with a broom, a technology that hasn't changed much in several thousand years, and doing so in a handmade home, which I can see no reason to leave until the day I go feet-first, feel like such blessings! And enjoying the least things—a chill glass of water, a moment of play with the cat, the sight of sunlight caught in the frost spangling the locust twigs—is a form of prayer.

Tamarack City's late postmaster once told me he thought my little house back here in the woods looked like a broody hen. It's where I try to create my own reality because, as my learned friend Doc Holliday once remarked, "normal reality is not all that commendable in any of its features that I can figure out." The house is just the right size: 720 square feet, with a single-pitch roof. The tall wall, 20 feet high, faces south with three good-sized windows and a sliding glass door. The short wall,

10 feet high, presents a small face to the north. Its two medium-sized windows flank the entryway and vestibule, which have salvaged doors with beveled glass panes. These front doors are on the house's north–south meridian, along with the cobble hearth, woodstove, and brick chimney, which is inside. The woodstove doors' glass inset lets firelight dance all the way out through the entry doors' panes and prisms, making a gladsome, welcoming sight, especially in winter.

Ordinarily, winters here are snowy but not severely cold. The house is snugly built, heated by wood, sunshine, and on rare occasions a small electric heater. It's well insulated, and all the big windows are double-glazed. There's no thermostat, just a sheet steel stove and a circulating fan. As the climate has changed and our summers have become warmer, a few portable electric fans have helped temper the hottest days. Insulated shades on all the windows also help moderate the temperature inside. I'm frugal with both the wood heat and the synthetic summer breezes. My house boasts electric lighting and indoor plumbing. Other modern conveniences include a refrigerator, a range, and a fuel-conserving demand-activated water heater, all of which burn bottled propane.

The vestibule-cum-mudroom has built-in recycling bins with space underneath for my vast, graceless array of outdoor footgear. I'm just a countrified, down-at-the-heels, scuffed-at-the-toes Imelda Marcos, walking in and out of two or three different pairs of shoes a day. I have aged hiking boots useful for wood splitting, rubber-and-leather oxfords for mud walking, plastic clogs for warm, wet weather walking, cross-country ski boots, lightweight snow boots, heavyweight snow boots, and decrepit Converse low-tops for painting and other such chores. In the space not given over to shoes and recyclables, there's a broom closet and a coat rack with a shelf overhead for my rustic millinery, the cataloging of which I'll spare the reader.

An east–west interior wall separates the guest room, the hallway-with-closet leading to the bathroom, and the vestibule from the rest of the house, which is open. The east wall accommodates bookshelves and cupboards and is home to a hi-fi system consisting of a turntable, a radio receiver, a tape deck, an amplifier, and two speakers. For Christmas 2001, a friend gave me a portable compact disc player that's become part of the array. There's no television set, no videocassette recorder, no digital versatile disc player at my house. My home entertainment center consists of a prodigal library, piles of magazines, the sound system, a few stitching projects, a picture window looking back into my thirty-five acres of wildlife habitat, and a cat, Simone De Fone Bone, who has been with me these past fifteen years.

Although not having television shouldn't seem that strange, more than once I've had to beat back offers of gift television sets, so it must look like a lack. My personal reasons for television avoidance are several. The most embarrassing is that when I'm in its presence, I can't take my eyes off it. Because advertising, the real content of television, is despicable, and because much of the ostensible content, the programming, is facile at best, after a spell of compulsive channel-surfing, I wind up feeling like a dope. Also, I remember how undiverting bedside television proved at the outset of my hospitalization following the automobile accident. There I lay, in a world of hurt, healing slowly, while on the screen men were casually beating one another up and then getting the girl and going out to dinner afterward. Cut, bruised, and busted up as I was, that faked violence was so painful to me that I couldn't watch it. I didn't need it then, and I don't need a wide-screen, high-resolution digital version of it now.

The hawking of communication technologies and consumer electronics to middle-class households has succeeded so
thoroughly that a person has only to forgo a few of the basics,
like the television set and the personal computer, to be swirled
off into a side eddy, there to remain, media-stagnant, as the
mainstream rushes swiftly onward. It's far too easy to qualify
as an eccentric nowadays.

The unavoidable truth is that to live simply, one must draw
the line somewhere against the consumer goods and gadgets
being urged upon us at every turn. A refusal to cross the line
into cyberspace automatically earns one the Luddite epithet.
Actually, I regard *Luddite* as an honorific. The original Luddites were loom-breakers in early-nineteenth-century Britain,
"rebels against the future," as Kirkpatrick Sale characterizes
them in his book of that title. They were cottagers who sup-
plemented their household subsistence with money earned by
weaving and knitting for the cotton trades on simple looms
and other machines in their homes. In the advent of the
Industrial Revolution, with its factory system and its drive to
consolidate and speed up the clothing industry through intensive mechanization, the Luddites rightly foresaw a mortal
threat to their way of life. Claiming the mythical Ned Ludd as
their general, they mounted a clandestine campaign of sabo-
tage against the largest mills. The Luddites' insurrection lasted
less than a year and was met with massive police and military
reprisal. They were hanged or transported for their resistance
of technology claiming to be progress.

In my retro-Luddite cottage, narrow stairs lead up to a
sleeping loft seven and three-fourths feet wide by thirteen and
one-half feet long, with a half-wall to the west for privacy. The
boudoir's appointments include a mattress and box spring, a
handmade birch nightstand, two lamps, a chest of drawers that
was new in 1958, and an armchair, now in its third coat of

upholstery, from my parents' home. The hand-me-down clock radio is vintage 1984.

My house is furnished largely with books and gifts; there's the hand-me-down furniture from Mom and Dad, photographs and drawings done by friends, and what was once crassly referred to as "wedding loot," including some first-rate chef's knives defaulted to me in Phil's remarkably nongrasping departure from the domicile prior to our divorce. There are pots and pans and lamps and dishes that I've been using since 1969, when I fixed up my first apartment after college. Some things in the house were bought new: the mattress and box spring, the couch, and the woodstove.

All these objects have a patina of associations. The fern in the corner of the bedroom was my first houseplant, acquired in 1969 from the Woolworth store at 40th and Telegraph in Oakland, California, right near the half-basement I shared with a friend from Phoenix. On the wall opposite the bed is a pen-and-ink drawing of a classical heroine climbing a tree, her grasp magically extended to reach a golden apple. This was a gift from the artist, Kathleen O'Neill, who was art director at *CoEvolution Quarterly* during my tenure there. Hanging over the half-wall is a Navajo saddle blanket from my father's family's days in Gallup, New Mexico. Before I made off with it, Dad was using this textile to cover a big tool in his wood shop, so I suspect that the Millses got it to use under a saddle and not as a curio.

East of the hearth, under the sleeping loft, is the living room, furnished with the now-dilapidated couch, another repeatedly reupholstered occasional chair of Mom and Dad's, two meditation cushions whose sole use is as extra seating, a footstool, a clever little folding rocker that was a hand-me-down from a friend, and the aforementioned sound system.

Southwest of the hearth is the dining area. It's high-ceilinged and lit by a rice-paper globe chandelier. There's a mahogany veneer china cabinet, bought at some friends' garage sale. It holds a few place settings of my grandmother's china, an assortment of hereditary serving pieces, and some of the wedding loot. The wobbly wooden dining table belonged to my neighbor Peggy's mother and has been on long-term loan in my place for more than a decade. From a friend going out of the restaurant business, I got eight beechwood Windsor chairs.

The half-alcove, half-island kitchen is in the northeast corner of the house, opposite the dining area. In the alcove are cupboards and countertops, open shelves, a brand-new demand water heater, and my second secondhand gas refrigerator. Pots and pans hang from the alcove's opening. On the west side of the kitchen, under a window, a stainless steel dual sink is positioned for scenic dishwashing. A half-wall surrounding the cupboards and counters that flank the secondhand gas range divides the kitchen from the dining area.

The kitchen is mostly equipped with hand tools. In the matter of wedding presents, Phil and I were ecological, if gauche. Through our parents, we let it be known that we preferred not to be given electric appliances as gifts. Prior to that, I'd accumulated a Cuisinart food processor, a citrus juicer, a hand mixer, a blender, and a toaster, all of which I employ from time to time. Life without the hand-me-down Electrolux vacuum cleaner would be dustier and quieter. I've got no microwave oven, no dishwasher, no trash masher, no washer-dryer combo. I have my laundry done in town.

Separate from the house, I have a writing studio, an eight-by-twelve-foot cell built a few years before the main house. When Phil and I began our five years together, as Rob's roommates, I moved into Phil's room, which was itself about eight by twelve, with one desk that we shared none too successfully. I badgered Phil to build me a work space, and before long he did, with some fresh lumber for framing and flooring and a lot of salvaged components, such as windows, doors, and paneling.

Since 1987, my studio has been the garment I don when I'm working. It contains, of course, a plethora of books, along with a couch, a door-desk resting on file cabinets, three lamps, and a small electric heater. Any wall space not occupied by bookshelves is hung with memorabilia, quotes, posters, poems, and souvenirs—things meaningful to me but too funky or junky to display in the house.

A picture window looks south, its view of an old field being steadily obscured by the growth of two maple trees that were mere saplings when the studio was placed here. In accordance with my Luddism, there is no computer in my studio or anywhere else on the premises. Later in this book, I'll discuss that choice more fully. It's in keeping with the precept that the fewer machines in my life, the better, especially machines that are not reparable and are scheduled for obsolescence.

One such that I do have, it behooves me to confess, is a fax machine. This acquisition cost me humanly because it meant fewer chatty encounters with Bernie the storekeeper over in Pineville. Before I got my own, Bernie's grocery's public fax came in handy in a pinch, as on one ferociously wintery day, at the height of a serious snowstorm, when I needed to send a fax. I gingerly drove the three miles to Bernie's through all the drifts and whiteouts. When I arrived, I saw Bernie coming down the cross street in his apron, jacket, and cap. Once we were both in the store, he told me he'd been delivering bottled water and a quart of milk to an old man up the street. Bernie knew that the man had fallen in his house a week before and didn't want anyone to know. So when he called, Bernie insisted on taking those necessities to him and, I guess, thought he could leave the store unattended for a few minutes with nothing to fear. There was, after all, a hellacious blizzard going on. I wouldn't want to have missed that glimpse of small-town kindness and Bernie's good example.

A long and persistent tradition argues against the technologies that supplant skill, neighborliness, good work, and, increasingly, mere employment. Around the world, activists from the original Luddites to Gandhi, and authors from Lewis Mumford to Chellis Glendinning and Ivan Illich, have questioned the morality of certain technologies and of the technologically mediated life; they have questioned the myths and merits of progress and modernity. However marginalized such thought and work remains, this questioning won't go away.

Convenience is nowhere on the list of the cardinal virtues. Temperance, prudence, fortitude, charity, justice, faith, and hope were what Socrates, Plato, and Saint Ambrose thought virtue hinged upon, not ease of operation or disposability. Is it possible that the proposition of being human is so different in our time as to have rendered those old virtues irrelevant? Questions like this, not all of them quite so rhetorical, confront me as I sit at my desk, trying to write.

On the windowsill before me is a de facto altar. It consists of a circle of bones, including a bird's skull, brought back from walks. To the right, in a small silver frame, is a snapshot of my mother offering a bright look and a tentative smile to some unseen guest in the receiving line at my wedding. Next to Mom is a cast brass Kwan Yin, the Chinese Buddhist goddess of mercy; next to her are a miniature Hano clown kachina doll, then an inch-high relief of what I take to be a future Buddha, a simple carved wood rabbit holding a flute, and a Crow Mother kachina doll, Angwúsnasomtaqa.

"The Crow Mother Kachina . . . is a beautiful and majestic figure," notes Frank Waters in *Book of the Hopi:*

> Two large crow wings stick out from the sides of her blue mask, which is tufted with breath-feathers and carries as face markings two inverted black triangles. . . .
>
> At the sunrise of the 20th day after her marriage to another Kachina, her brother, according to custom, was bringing her back in her wedding clothes from the home of the groom's parents . . . to her own family home. At this moment, she received the urgent call from the Hopi people, requesting her assistance at the Powamu ceremony. . . . Her song tells the Kachina clan migration story. She ends it with a long sigh . . . meaning that she has traveled a long way and is very tired.

The Powamu ceremony is a part of the Hopi people's cycle of nine religious ceremonies—profound mystery plays that, in Water's words, "dramatize the universal laws of life."

The Kachinas are spirits that come to help the agricultural Hopi people with all aspects of their lives, lives once lived in the omnipresence of the sacred. Kachina dolls are effigies of these tutelary helpers. Originally, the dolls were made for Hopi children as part of their religious education. Now, many dolls are made as souvenirs or collector's items. My doll is crudely made, a souvenir. Kachina dolls were part of my childhood, too. I was ignorant of their religious significance but drawn to them nonetheless.

That the Crow Mother's journey home is interrupted by a people's call for help, and that the help is given in part by the telling of an origin story, makes her doll a fitting object for a writer's desk, I think. She hastened to serve, didn't even pause to change out of her wedding dress.

Other images pinned to the window frame above my altar include a postcard of a nineteenth-century New Mexican death cart effigy, a grinning skeleton seated in a wooden cart, bow drawn, arrow nocked. There's a postcard image of a thirteenth-century sandstone statue of the Hindu god Ganesha, the jelly-bellied, dreadlocked, elephant-headed son of Shiva and Parvati. Another authorial divinity, Ganesha broke off the end of one of his tusks and used it to write later sections of the Mahabharata, one of the two great Sanskrit epics of India. With his elephantine strength, Ganesha is Hinduism's lord of beginnings and remover of obstacles and is called upon for help in completing huge, difficult projects—like books, or sinks full of dirty dishes.

Next to the Crow Mother is a quirky little doll that Phil brought back from a trip to British Columbia for the Third North American Bioregional Congress. The doll's head and torso consist of a three-inch cylindrical section of an antler. Four stubby, paddle-shaped pieces of antler, attached to the doll's body by two strings threaded through it, make the doll's arms and legs; they rattle like dry bones when I shake the doll. The doll's face consists of three drill holes: two eyes set on either side of a blunt nose, and a mouth permanently agape in alarm, dismay, or worry beneath those staring, hollow eyes. Its expression, Phil said, had reminded him of me.

The reasons for viewing with alarm seem to have multiplied, but on the page and through the window, across the threshold of the studio, the manifestations of beauty and interest, the realities to savor and occasions for gratitude, proliferate, too.

That chance assemblage of images and effigies holds the foreground of my writing realm. They're not quite idols or household gods but emblems of mysteries. They, too, offer some wisdom on the question of how we are to live.

3

SPRING

Spring is never of a sameness. There is stimulus in its caprices, as on a gusty, partly cloudy day when the sun plays hide-and-go-seek. The warmth harries snow from its last shady hideouts. The dance of spring is a do-si-do, with snow melting and snow falling, warmth coaxing and chill betraying. Patience with the ratty weather wears thin. Walks out back are full of breaking news. The fresh-bared earth reeks of Eros.

What spring brings of its own accord is the fact and parable of resurgence and the counsel to seize the day. When the snow departs, it goes unevenly, leaving an Appaloosa landscape. Under the hardwoods, the longer, warmer days will coax hepaticas, spring beauties, Dutchman's-breeches, and violets out from under their mulch of fallen leaves. The delicacy and the surety of the wildflowers' comeback gently calls pessimism into question.

Limbering up, the crows—companionable, intelligent, artic-ulate, and ubiquitous—engage in airborne frolics. As the grainy old snow recedes, the expanses of rank brown mottling the field, their color tinctured from the million bowed weeds, gobble the sun's warmth and spread. Half a dozen crows alight and forage, picking at the matted stems and leaves.

In addition to the resident crows, migratory birds begin to return. The year-round chickadees seem friendly as always, and the bees are out and about. All these life-forms make good company; I regard them as fellow souls, which makes me an animist. Animism is the oldest—as in Stone Age—old-time religion. My spirituality is parochial, terrestrial. I do qualify as a W.I.T.C.H. (Woman Interested in Talking to Crows and Herbs), but my irregular practice and impromptu rituals don't aim at producing any dramatic results except, perhaps, in me. Saluting the wild things is simple decorum.

The crows are a great tribe, persecuted but unvanquished. The corvid nation includes ravens, crows, and jays, the smartest of birds. Their actions and speech are varied and complex. Crow talk bespeaks curiosity and sociability, even superciliousness. Occasionally I hear what I take to be a raven quarking in the pines behind the house. Maybe it nests somewhere out back, or perhaps my place is on its regular beat. I try to talk with it and with the crows from time to time, but I think these birds must hear my callings and croakings as Parisians hear my French—as a risible effrontery: "Don't try to speak to me in my tongue. I'll lurch along in yours, you silly."

The corvids' presence year-round keeps my ears pricked. If those corvids happen to be Eastern blue jays, their cries of alarm mean "Look up!" and may warn of a raptor sailing above, menacing all the many winged and furred morsels. As the snow melts, so does an architectural medium; the subniveal runways of mice, voles, and other little rodents are unroofed, exposing their denizens to the hungers of birds of prey and other plunderers.

Walking south from my studio through the field, I see these mouse trails and, stirred into activity by the sun, one of the foot-high anthills that hunkers at the base of the palisade of spruces walling the field's east edge. The aboveground ants mass in shadows cast by the spruces' boughs, teeming in the shade. A few squads and individuals venture out into the full sun.

Juncos in the nearby fringe of Scotch pines pour out rills of song, gladdening the air. Dozens of them fly out and casually settle themselves across a small stretch of the moss- and lichen-covered tundra at the foot of the spruce stand. Mole-gray except for their charcoal executioner's hoods and white outer tail feathers, the juncos hop and hunt, dispersed across the territory, until they notice the cat and then whirl up en masse like last year's leaves caught in a sudden gust.

The less adaptable birds, which is to say most of them, are experiencing difficulty in coexisting with an ever-expanding human presence. According to Edward O. Wilson's *Diversity of Life*, for instance, "from the 1940s to the 1980s, population densities of migratory songbirds in the mid-Atlantic United States dropped 50%, and many species became locally extinct."

Such sad truths mean that when spring still adds, day by day, more songs to the overall erotic clamor, its perennial quality of surprise is heightened by a feeling of reprieve. My mind may dwell overmuch on the extinction crises being perpetrated by civilization, but I cannot deny the evidence of nature's enormous will to flourish. The adaptable birds are still nesting. Reduced in diversity, life goes on nonetheless. Behind the house, a pair of eastern blue jays arc through the twisty boughs of the Scotch pines, clucking connubially as they wing through the scrub to select only the best twigs for nest construction. Are these the jays or the offspring of the jays I saw enacting these mysteries last year?

The festival of their return prompts me to unravel a defunct sweater and donate snipped bits of its yarn, along with scraps of ribbon, string too short to save, and cotton from vitamin bottles, for their nesting endeavor. I please myself and maybe the jay birds by festooning the locust tree with these offerings to their futurity. Call it northern hospitality.

"Writers are magpies," says my bioregionalist friend Peter Berg, alluding to this corvid's trait of fancying and absconding with odd items, especially things that glitter. Along with their good-time kleptomania, magpies grab and mimic things they hear. The chief totems of writers, however, must be the Mimidae, the mockingbird family, with their showy polyglot songs. The mockingbird's song was a music of my childhood. When I return to Arizona and hear the mockingbirds sing, I have to wonder about their influence and my penchant for splendiferous vocabulary.

There comes a time near the vernal equinox when robins are everywhere, chirping their simple, hearty song. Not long thereafter, I may glimpse a pair of brown thrashers just in front of the studio, investigating the undersides of leaves and litter and then prudently returning to their covert in the ground-sweeping branches of the pines. Where I live, these handsome rufous mimic thrushes are the mockingbirds' prominent kin. Although at present the brown thrasher is neither endangered nor threatened, it is a country bird whose survival in local populations and as a species is contingent on the survival of the scrub and brush habitat it finds in rural areas.

Rain or shine, thrashers seem to revel in spring and are happy to say so. Early on, I may hear a thrasher singing outside the bedroom window, plagiarizing several other birds'

songs, including the phoebe's raspy name-saying. Phoebes are to thrashers as cymbals are to orchestras. Phoebes get their point across instantly, whereas thrashers invite close listening. If thrashers choose to nest nearby, their exuberant songs will underscore the whole of spring and early summer.

On certain days in certain Mays, thanks to some combination of inspiration and atmospheric conditions, the thrashers' vocalizing sounds magically clean and reverberant. On those occasions one might, with real birding skill, be able to distinguish among individual thrashers by recognizing their different medleys. Lady thrashers, of course, are naturally endowed with such discernment.

Late one May in the cherry grove to the west of my studio, I listened to a thrasher belting out his composite song. This bird and his paternal ancestors—indeed, all the brown thrasher fellows—have listened to all the other birdsongs around them and composed their favorite measures into busy freshets of doubled phrases uniquely their own. In this thrasher's song I thought I heard catbird, cardinal, and wood thrush, along with a possible half-dozen other birdsongs that I couldn't identify.

Although the thrashers' bird-land song swings, it's no lullaby, but often peals forth as the morning sun is rising. It's about rousing, not lulling, which makes it a serenade. From a top branch in the big cherry tree that looms north of my studio, the thrashers' multiplicitous, felicitous song is one of the joyfullest noises of spring, a heraldic fantasia learned from father by son, perhaps to be tweaked by the younger generations' inclusion of songs, and just sounds, from the world around.

Small wonder that the singing of the brown thrasher throws a gauntlet in the path of the bird-watching prose-meister. Writers sweat to rival the birds' paeans. Edward Howe Forbush, in

his lovely, old-fashioned *Natural History of American Birds of Eastern and Central North America,* quotes fellow enthusiast Simeon Pease Cheney's description of the brown thrasher's performance:

> The first eccentric accent compels us to admit that the spirit of song has fast hold on him. As the fervor increases, his long and elegant tail droops. His whole plumage is loosened and trembling. His head is raised and his bill is wide open; there is no mistake; it is the power of the god.

In my attempt to portray the thrasher, lyric envy prompted me to seek elsewhere than metaphysics for a metaphor. Maybe thrashers are scat singing, I thought. Thus my question, an instance of nature writing at its coziest, took me to the jazz shelf of the local library. Magpies play with what catches their eye, and writers forage where their fancy takes them. In search of the definitive word on scat, I turned to Langston Hughes' *First Book of Jazz,* where I read:

> Sometimes for fun, singers sing "oo-yah-koo" syllables to boppish backgrounds today as Cab Calloway in the 1930s sang "hi-de-hi-de-ho-de-hey," meaning nothing, or as Lionel Hampton sang, "hay-baba-re-bop" in 1940, or as Louis Armstrong used to sing "scat" syllables to his music in Chicago in the 1920s, or as Jelly Roll Morton shouted meaningless words to ragtime music in the early 1900s, or as the Mother Goose rhyme said, "Hey diddle-diddle, the cat and the fiddle," even before that—for fun. Nonsense syllables are not new in poetry or music, but they are fun.

And, Hughes concludes, "Jazz *is* fun."

My metaphor quest suddenly broadened into a reflection on human history and the parallels between slavery and the human use of nature. The earth still manages to engender beauty despite all the exploitation. African people, despite

their enslavement in America, created an entirely new art form under the sun. Improvisational, imaginative, jazz is fun, and jazz is a phoenix bird. Jazz and blues constitute the great American contribution to world culture. They originate in a genius persisting through a history of captivity, slavery, overt persecution, institutional racism, tacit discrimination, and tireless, perilous resistance, manifesting tremendous humanity every step of the way. Jazz voices that unvanquishable, natural will toward creativity and self-expression, despite everything, in the here and the now. Jazz is a great invention to tell this truth: There is no survival without joy, without lamentation; no being without rhythm, play, and song.

Learning more about scat, and about the thrashers' talent for artful quotation, persuaded me not to liken elements of a thrasher's serenade to nonsense syllables. For the various singers the thrasher flatters sincerely by his imitation, these bits and pieces of birdsong have definite meaning. According to Darwin's clean logic, male birds' songs generally mean "Oo, baby, I'm unattached, strong and healthy, and lookin' to reproduce. Over here!" Or they may mean "This is our pad (territory). Beat it (kindly go elsewhere)." Most birdsong is no-nonsense communication.

When the thrasher's top forty reprises other species' songs, female birds of those other species, scientists say, are not fooled. They know their own kind. The point is not deception or evasion, and thus it is not mimicry in its exactest sense. Why, then, biologists have to wonder, does Mr. *Toxostoma rufum* build such a big song catalog? Ah, it has to do with reproductive fitness, or what we nonbiologists term sex appeal. Presumably, the fact that a bird and his forebears live long enough to appropriate a rich array of sounds (for not all Mimidae material is avian song) evidences wit and health and stoutness of gonads. Ms. Thrasher, wanting only the sturdiest

antecedents for her fledglings, will try to hitch up with a singer
with a worldly air. Her interest piqued, say the books, she will
offer her tawny-feathered Bobby McFerrin a twig. One twig
leads to another, and the next thing you know the thrashers are
building a cup-shaped nest close to the ground in a thicket,
filling it to capacity with four to five pale bluish or greenish
eggs, rearing their young, and fulfilling another cycle of lives.
When autumn approaches, they will head south to winter in
slightly warmer reaches of North America—places such as
Georgia, which claims the brown thrasher as its state bird.

Given the existential meaning of the thrasher's vocal
appropriations, I was forced, finally, to relinquish scat singing
as my metaphor. What in the realm of jazz, where I was wintering, might say it? Is the thrasher riffing, stringing licks
together? A riff, according to Mervyn Cooke's *Jazz*, is "essen-
tially a simple but catchy melodic motif repeated over and over
again (known in classical music as an *ostinato*, from the Italian
word for obstinate)."

At times, the thrasher's relentless vocalizing amply conveys
his stubbornness of intent, and any male bird's song might
fairly be called his licks. This jazz invention stems from the
genius of Louis Armstrong, whose playing, wrote Cooke, "was
characterized by a wide variety of original melodic and tempo
devices that make his style instantly recognizable. Comparable
formulae (subsequently known as 'licks' or 'signatures') would
be used by countless later musicians as personal identifiers."

Out in the open-air concert hall, when the thrasher is done
riffing for the day, the other songsters get in their licks. It is the
crow's turn to shout and the neighbors' rooster's turn to crow.
In the background, there is the sound of applause, last year's
dried beech leaves clapping lightly in the stiff southwest wind.

Whether the nights are freezing or no, by May it is irrev-
ocably spring, with cool, moist morning air fresh and fragrant

with just-turned soil and new-mown grass. Early on, the serviceberries flower. The leaves of the pin cherry trees—limpid,
radiant blades imbued with rosy light—are out. Maple and
beech leaf buds, too, swell and unfurl with that same nubile
life, while the wild cherry flower buds still clench like minuscule fists. The presence of a thousand tender shades of green,
of more bursts of white blossoms, of bees in a nectaring frenzy,
adds to the mounting joy of the birds' giving rise to new generations of jays, thrashers, robins, and chickadees. It is a
mighty salute to the life force, the planet's resounding improv-
isations in the key of *Be*.

The marvels have started. Migratory and dormant life-
forms have returned or roused themselves, feasting the ears,
giving the sense of hearing more to attend than growling
gear-changes of distant, heavy trucks. The soil has thawed,
the blood is stirred, and hemoglobin hankers for chlorophyll.

Well before the meltdown, though, the seed catalogs,
earliest signs of spring, will have arrived. Page upon colorful
page of apotheoses of eggplant, tomato, and lettuce excite an
eagerness in me to get out and grow some of these paragons
myself. Gardening bestrides more seasons than spring. Imagining the garden begins long before the vernal equinox.
Preparing the soil and starting seeds can begin as soon as the
snow is gone. Most of the daily tending takes place during
summer, with harvesting and weeding continuing into the
fall, or so they tell me. I'm a sporadic and not hugely successful gardener. I keep making my attempts, partly for fun,
mostly from a sense of obligation. Vegetable gardening is
necessary and interesting, and mine someday may even be
productive. Patience is called for. Building the soil in which

to garden is a long-term proposition, whether it is a forest, a prairie, or a householder doing it.

The obligation to at least try to grow some of my own food was borne in on me several years ago in Austin, Texas, at a talk given by Oren Lyons, faith-keeper of the Turtle clan of the Onondaga Nation. Lyons is what Anglos call a chief, although the Indian word, *hoyawnah*, for such a position means "the good mind." *Good mind* suits him. Lyons is a man worth listening to, I had learned some twenty years ago at a conference in which we both participated. There, in a disquisition on the governance of the Iroquois confederacy and much else besides, Lyons said a couple of things, almost in passing, that have stayed with me ever since. "Much will be asked of those to whom much has been given," he said, investing me with an abiding sense of *bourgeois oblige,* and "Don't look for mercy where there is none," which has led me to try not to waste too much thought or energy on reformist strategies. Lyons' mercy maxim is the reason why I'm a Luddite. Looking to certain systems and their infrastructures—such as capital-intensive factory farming, an agriculture dependent on chemical inputs, herbicides, genetically manipulated organisms, and pesticides—for ecological mercy is as pointless as hoping that the brown bear whose territory you've carelessly entered will be a vegetarian.

Chancing into his talk at the University of Texas, I was more than willing to let Oren Lyons inform my life again. The discomforting maxim in this talk was that "only the people who know how to plant and grow food are going to make it through the coming hard times." Given the degree of ecological and cultural disturbance that prevails on earth, why wouldn't hard times be coming? Indeed, for an increasing proportion of the world's people, hard times are here. Human numbers grow. More people are displaced from land or employment. Land itself is ruined, built over, ripped up, eroded into desert. Inequity increases. In the wake of the industrial era's greedy, wasteful folly, it is not just the practical ability to tend the soil and produce food that will reemerge as fundamental to a sustainable, simpler way of life. A humbling and a willingness to kneel down and touch the ground will be critical, too. However estranged from these realities we may be today, we need to recall that all flesh is grass, that our lives, too, stem from the soil.

If long-term survival supplies one major incentive to garden, peer pressure is another. Where I live, it's embarrassing not to have a vegetable garden. By summertime, one is supposed to be palming off zucchini on all passersby. When Phil and I began our new home, one of the first things we did was to start a little garden. For the first couple of years, the site, a small opening in the pines below the house, was good. This probably had to do with the truckload of rotted pig manure tilled into it.

The summer of the divorce, the garden was spectacular. Phil was long gone—off to the Caribbean with Megan, who would become his new wife and fellow topsoil builder. His old wife, meanwhile, feeling scorned and furious, threw herself into horticulture. I splurged on perennials, herbs, chives, and rhubarb plants. I purchased deluxe seeds, bought vegetable starts. Every day I weeded, keeping my garden perfect while the imperfection of other quarters of my life glared every time a letter from the attorneys hashing out our split-up detonated.

By harvest time that year, my mood had improved. The divorce was done, and I was having an affair with the contractor who was completing the detail work on the house. Harry was a deluxe guy, an aikido practitioner, Zen student, beekeeper, and guitarist accomplished in many genres—altogether a smart, funny, good-hearted man. For the couple of months when he was working around the place, we'd been having enjoyable conversations. By and by, one twig led to another. Our liaison, an outcome of attraction and propinquity, seemed only natural. As autumn approached, it was my delight to feed Harry dishes prepared from the day's freshly picked vegetables. I might harvest a couple of cucumbers, a handful of bush beans, and two handfuls of potatoes and cook the bounty forthwith, being careful not to steam the potatoes a second too long or to overseason the cucumber salad.

The following spring, I began a coast-to-coast hegira as a roving bioregionalist, promoting my first book, attending conferences, and visiting old friends. The garden, neglected in my frequent absences, went to hell, as did the affair with Harry.

When the next gardening season rolled around, I found I'd lost my zeal for the old garden site. Perhaps I'd tilled in a little too much spite. I also had to admit that however historic, the location was not propitious; it was low-lying, shaded increasingly by the growing pines, and the last place near the house to be freed of snow. Because what's underfoot here is not so much soil as sand, that dose of fertility recruited from an old pigpen had been quickly exhausted.

For the next couple of years, I didn't have a garden. I kept telling myself that the thing to do would be terrace the sunnier, southeast-facing slope in front of my studio. There I could start anew and resume the topsoil-building endeavor. In this scheme, I'd have garden beds handy to tend whenever the writing got impossible. During those years, I found myself traveling, often during spring and summer, as I worked on another book. The bold new beginning in the better location remained but a vision.

After a while, there was a new man in my life. Tom enjoyed both gardening and cooking. Over at his place he had a big garden, cunningly furnished with found-art trellises, borders, and mulches made from materials that less frugal folk had discarded. For me to have a garden seemed redundant. I could work a bit in Tom's garden to earn a serving or two of fresh vegetables: do a little weeding or pick the beans and lettuce for our supper.

After I'd been a migrant laborer at his place for a couple of years, Tom said he wanted me to have the fun of a garden of my own. That June, he announced that his garden was already overrun with plants. He sought a sunny venue where his surplus cucurbits and solanums could indulge their expansionist tendencies. He would plant some squash and tomatoes on my sandy studio slope with its southern exposure. In his station wagon he hauled buckets of horse manure over to my place. He fertilized a little plot and then installed the half-dozen or so plants he'd lovingly started. Now all I had to do was look after this kindly gift of a garden.

After a week or so, Tom mentioned that he thought that shallow watering, which is what he had noticed me doing, causes vegetable roots to linger near the surface, where they're likely to dry out. Deep watering in big soaks, he said, lures the roots down into the soil, sends them questing with gravity for the moisture at depth. A leaky bucket, he said, could be an economical means of such slow and steady drip irrigation.

Shortly after receiving that advice, I was headed out to my writing studio to put my pert nose to the literary grindstone. Suddenly I felt myself overpowered by an urge to do some deep watering. As a side benefit of my involvement with the local natural foods cooperative, I am the possessor of several five-gallon white plastic buckets that once contained peanut butter and other bulk food items. I figured I could spare one for drip watering. As I pierced a bucket near the bottom with five closely spaced nail holes, it occurred to me that in many parts of the world, water vessels are often a family's most essential piece of household goods; to have an extra bucket to perforate seemed to me a form of wealth.

From the faucet by the side of the house, I filled two other buckets. When Phil and I built the house, the drilling company down the road had sunk a 200-foot-deep well and installed a submersible electric pump. A statewide utility supplies the energy to raise the water from such a depth. I turn the tap and cold, clean, potable water gushes forth. This water came easy.

"Use it up, wear it out, make do, or do without" is one old formula for material simplicity and nonconsumerism. Lacking sufficient garden hose and being too cheap to buy any, I spent the afternoon hauling buckets of water from the tap to Tom's squash and tomato plantation.

Water is heavy. Carrying the weight got me thinking about all the effort expended all around the world on hand-watered crops. Gaining sympathy with peasant women everywhere, I made it a discipline to carry two full five-gallon buckets nonstop the 200 yards from the tap to the thirsty pumpkins. Carrying water pained my palms, felt as if it were dragging my arms out of their sockets, and bore me down to the ground. When I put the buckets down, my arms would float up involuntarily, as they do in that kids' trick after one has pressed outward on a door frame for a minute with the backs of the hands. When carrying water and chopping wood is not a choice but a necessity, it's toil that can break people down, bend them over for life. Members of the middle class might imagine that peasants would cultivate strength and fortitude along with crops and other bare necessities, but what if that's not so? What if that mandatory simplicity just leaves folk weary and aching all the time?

It may be that humanity took a wrong turn with the invention of agriculture. There's probably no turning back, but forensic anthropologists now tell us that, contrary to popular belief, once crops were domesticated and could be stored, human health declined as settlements developed and human populations rose. Thinkers such as Paul Shepard say that our psyches also took a wrong turn back then. In *The Tender Carnivore and the Sacred Game,* Shepard argues that the domestication of organisms and civilization's misunderstanding of and alienation from nature are cause and effect. Domesticated plants and animals are a debased, infantilized version of wild stocks. The pastoral misleads us as to the nature of Nature, which is wild.

Still, a woman's got to eat, and even Oren Lyons says that food comes from those who plant and grow it. My friend Deering, who nearly always gets his buck, says that if for some apocalyptic reason we all decide to revert to foraging, "there'll be one hunt and one gather."

Having mused my way full circle from the old Stone Age to the new, I placed the perforated bucket at the first squash plant and filled it to the brim. The water sprinkled out at just the right rate of flow, filling the little well around the plant's stem without overspilling the berm. Eureka! Flushed with success, I was in my own personal Findhorn, bringing happiness and good wishes to vegetables along with precious water. These poor plants! Long on sunshine, short on humus, they were attempting to grow in ground either stark or mangy with knapweed, bunchgrass, and sorrel. It would take a mighty power of wishing to make this improbable garden succeed.

While waiting for the watering bucket to empty before moving to the next thirsty plant, I ripped up spotted knapweed wherever I saw it flower. In 1986 I first learned from some bioregionalist friends from British Columbia, who were having complicated troubles with knapweed invasions, what a demonic plant it can be. Battling knapweed became my hopeless crusade. Friends here were insouciant. Harry valued it as a honey plant for his bees. Sue, a landscape architect, bioregionalist, and ace vegetable gardener, thought it beautiful when fields dominated by knapweed burst into lavender bloom. Peggy imagined that the knapweed infestation would run its course eventually. Surely it must be doing something worthwhile, or it wouldn't be there in the first place.

I, meanwhile, was compiling a dossier on the evils of spotted knapweed. *Centaurea maculosa,* a very tough cousin to the bachelor's button, is a weed genius. It flourishes on disturbed ground, possessing an array of talents that allow it quickly to dominate any expanse of untended open land it meets. Its composite flowers produce seed copiously, and its seeds are among the first to germinate in spring. The plants flower early and continue to bloom throughout the summer and fall. Knapweed is hardly discouraged by mowing. The plant has a long taproot and is allelopathic, meaning that it poisons the surrounding soil, making it inhospitable to other plants. All these traits have allowed knapweed to take over every old field, vacant lot, and roadside in my county. Worse, it's invading natural areas. Knapweed seeds hitchhike in pant cuffs, in Bowser's coat, and in the dirt caught on lug soles. Beach and woodland trails are hedged with knapweed now.

After Tom had pooh-poohed my knapweed pogrom, I asked him whether he had ever seen a knapweed that had been eaten by anything. He conceded that he had not. Eventually, though, something will show up to eat it. Some insect or bacterium will develop an appetite for knapweed, and the feasting will begin. Then we'll have to worry about what something that would eat knapweed might want for dessert. But "eventually" will be too late for the communities of plants and animals that knapweed displaces.

The number of knapweed plants on just my acreage is so vast, it's like the duration of a Hindu *kalpa:* vast as the number of grains of sand on the world's beaches or the number of seconds in a millennium. Over the years, as I've waged my losing battle, my choices have dwindled. In small areas, my current strategy is to uproot knapweed as it blooms and avert reproduction, especially by the big, brawny plants. I aim to cause some genetic enfeeblement and maintain a few knapweed-free zones around my home.

Returning to the watering, I moved the bucket to the next squash plant. There, the water broke the berm. Bare-handed, I scooped up some dirt and patted it into place so that the irrigation would proceed without waste. This action gave me something in common with every gardener who's ever hoed a little ditch to direct the water's flow. It brought to mind my friend Chellis Glendinning's descriptions of her village in northern New Mexico, where the customary water rights and collective governments of the acequias, or irrigation systems, are centuries old. I also thought of Ladakh, "Little Tibet" in the shadow of the Himalayas, where every day I watched a woman at the guest house where I was staying use a mattock to open and close a little runnel. Here, the meltwater is allocated to individual fields according to an ancient and elementary cooperative system. All over the world, people who know how to plant and grow food understand that water means life. If ways aren't found to conserve and share it, people will fight for water, to the death.

No water wars broke out on my turf, and thanks to all the tending, Tom's starter garden on the studio slope yielded two softball-sized pumpkins and a brace of green tomatoes. The tomato crop might have been more bountiful if I hadn't come reluctantly late to the necessity of killing the tomato horn-

worms. Any encounter with those grotesque, outsized caterpillars makes me glad that I stand more than five feet tall and
am not a photosynthesist.

However scanty the harvest, the tutorial value of this little
garden was great. Tom's gift prompted me to involve myself
with a patch of ground in that real world where humanity does
not live by books alone. Even a little bit of gardening reminded
me that labor informs the self as nothing else can. Proceeding
at a pace that permits craft and invention allows some connection with a great swath of human history.

That said, I still needed some prodding to stay with it. The
following year Peggy, without intending to, shamed me into
beginning another garden. Innocently enough, she offered me
some flower and vegetable starts when I stopped by her place
one Saturday. Little did I reckon what a fitting appellation
starts would prove to be.

Standing there opposite my spry, trim neighbor, looking
into her keen blue eyes, I started to decline her generosity.
"Oh, gee," I said, "thank you very much, but I've really got to
build some raised beds and terrace the hillside behind my studio and replumb the house so I can have a spigot closer, and,
and . . ."

"Why don't you just dig a hole and plant 'em in the
ground?" she wanted to know.

"I don't have a shovel," I said truthfully, having broken
mine a year or so before in a tree-planting extravaganza.

"You can borrow ours. We've got a spare."

Nothing remained but to take the shovel and the plants,
head over to the vicinity of my studio, and start gardening.
Although the results of the past year's garden had not been all
that encouraging, the fact remained that a few edibles had
grown there. The site has sunlight if nothing else. It is, as
remarked, a long haul from the water faucet. Garden hose is

fairly cheap, but rather than buying a few fathoms of hose, I'd had the notion that to maintain a good-sized garden, I would have to wait till I could afford to have a plumber install a faucet nearer the site. Hand-watering, for all its atavistic resonance, was not a practice I cared to sustain.

This year, one simple solution kept leading to the next and eventuated in my purchase of some garden hose. I had free plants and the loan of a tool. "What the heck," I thought, "I'll dig a few holes and help those starts commit suicide." Although their prospects looked dim, it seemed only fair to these aspiring vegetables to do some knapweed discouragement around their home-to-be. To expedite that task, I borrowed Peggy's lawn mower. I was pleased that I was able to get the mower going without having to get some big, strong man to yank on the starter cord for me, and I decapitated the knapweed already burgeoning all over the ten-by-fifteen-foot plot behind the studio.

Gratifying as mowing down lots of knapweed was, the end couldn't justify the means, and my conscience was troubled. In a world desperate for surcease from fossil fuel combustion and for more natural habitat, power lawn mowers are noisy pollution wagons; their use seems frivolous at best. It dawned on me that rather than continuing to mow the paths between the garden beds I'd plotted, I could mulch, using slabs from the straw bales that had insulated the base of my studio through the winter. I could smother the knapweed sprouts under a grid of straw, leaving yard-square openings for the vegetable plants.

Now the horticultural inspiration was coming fast and furious. I could give Peggy's plants a fighting chance and enrich these modest straw-cordoned plots with the compost that had for the past few years been accumulating down at the old garden site.

To prepare the compost, I decided I needed a coarse sieve, a riddle. At this point I was so brazen in my borrowing that I just walked over and helped myself to another of my neighbor's tools. Quite apart from its utility, a riddle is worth having for the pleasure of its good Old English name. In years past, when I'd hand-sifted soil or compost, I'd also riddled my Womanswork gloves in an afternoon. Once trimmed to size, a scrap of siding that had lain rotting for some years became a perfect squeegee to spare the gloves and work the compost through the screen.

I plunged Peggy's shovel into the compost heap and turned up dark, rich, clean soil. Minute alchemists had transformed an accumulation of rotted vegetable parings into a small garden's worth of good, sweet humus. I'd never had a vegetable garden before my move to the Midwest, but I had been a devout composter nonetheless. When I lived on Telegraph Hill, I hauled my weekly bucket of kitchen bio-waste to my workplace in Sausalito, where I handed it off to a colleague who lived in the country. He gardened and raised chickens and would from time to time give me a dozen eggs.

I ran my compost through the riddle to prepare it and remove the blue rubber bands from the bunches of scallions, the tea-bag strings and tags, the lumps of charcoal from dustpan emptyings. In the process, earthworms, principal authors of this humus, came to light. The crowd I run with tends to regard earthworms as culture heroes. Given the plenitude of garbage and the dwindling of the topsoil, any being that can turn garbage into soil deserves a measure of respect.

Imagine my dismay on learning that the presence of earthworms is not an unqualified boon. New research into earthworm ecology suggests that earthworms aren't native to the regions of North America that were covered by the ice sheet of the last glaciation. They couldn't have persisted in frozen soils, and they are slow travelers. Evidently the earthworms now in these parts rode in from Europe or Asia in potting soil rather than having moved northward with the retreat of the ice. A glacial pace is faster than an earthworm fauna. Ecologists speculate that the earthworm's rapid consumption and conversion of leaf litter on forest floors may be disrupting a lot of microhabitat there.

Be that as it may, I need these aliens for my horticultural purposes. I riddled carefully and scanned the compost for signs of movement or glistening skin. Some of the earthworms played possum until I plucked them from the screen and dropped them into the compost-hauling buckets, whereupon they sprang into action and crawled around the bottom of the bucket in spur-of-the-moment worm derbies. Making the personal acquaintance of many of the earthworms that would be burrowing into, aerating, and fertilizing the earth in the new garden had a nice collegial feel.

My cheap and primitive technique involved much shoveling and heavy lifting. Along with the compost screening, I was excavating these square plots in their ramparts of straw, sieving the weed-infested sand before hauling it away, and disposing of the knapweed, quack grass, St. John's wort, and peppergrass that had been rooted in it.

Here in the land of the short growing season, old-timers say you shouldn't set out your plants before Decoration (Memorial) Day. Given the rate at which I manage to get my garden sites ready, it's a wonder any of my plants make it outdoors before Halloween. The inconvenient thing about gardening, I find, is that I am not in charge of the timing. It is a seasonal activity involving sedentary beings whose flourishing depends on being in the right place at the right time.

While I bustled around making all the preparations I deemed necessary to setting them out, my trays full of free seedlings were getting awfully leggy. Squash especially are quick to grow into brawny plants all out of proportion to their cubicles in the propagation tray. It doesn't take very many weeks indoors for them to start looking as if they're becoming ingrown, yearning to break out and stretch their roots.

Finally planting out Peggy's flower and vegetable starts felt to me as I imagine it must to put one's kid on the school bus for the first time. I could only hope that these tender little beings would survive the transition to a harsher environment that includes deer, woodchucks, cottontails, tomato horn-worms, cabbage loopers, drought, and horticultural ineptitude. Under my concentration, what a weight of responsibility the simple gift of tomatoes, basil, zucchini, and cosmos had become! I felt as though I'd blithely adopted dozens of hungry, thirsty children whose insistent needs must be met else they'd perish, leaving their pathetic corpses to weigh on my con-science.

Most folks around here just get their eighth or sixteenth of an acre rototilled, fertilize it, and get on with the program. They dig holes and plant those seeds in the ground. It was, in a sense, a luxury for me to garden in this toilsome, inexpert fashion. As the toil continued while the amusement I got from doing it my way dwindled, I had my doubts. It's not as if I was hoping to get a blue ribbon for my Hubbard squashes at the county fair or expecting to save a bundle on groceries. Yet as the growing season progressed and the plants began rewarding me with a few tangy tomatoes, a cupful of basil leaves, and an ordinate number of zucchini, I was mighty pleased. The toil was forgotten. I had that getting-something-for-nothing thrill of plucking the fruit from the vine as easily as though the gates of Eden had never clanged shut. By trial and error, grace and idiosyncrasy, I was learning to plant and grow some food.

4

THE OTHERS

Several years ago, after I had completed a reading at an independent bookstore in northern California on a promotional tour, a teacher appeared—as in "When the student is ready, the teacher will appear."

The book I was promoting, *In Service of the Wild,* is about ecological restoration, the art and science of helping nature heal damaged land. Quite a lot of restoration work entails the removal of invasive alien species of plants and animals, imported or stowaway organisms such as kudzu, starlings, or knapweed, that can outcompete and overwhelm the less prolific, less adaptable members of native ecosystems.

During the discussion following the reading, an earnest, wired young man had described his progress in developing a backyard habitat that would be inviting to a broad range of native birds. His question concerned the native but aggressive blue jays. These avian generalists were beginning to elbow out the less common, less numerous birds he'd succeeded in attracting to his yard, and the question was what to do. I think this aspiring restorationist might have been looking to me for a dispensation to kill or somehow rout the jays. Here was a dilemma. I couldn't think of a good answer, but I didn't argue for the jays' right to life. I lamely advised him to let his conscience be his guide.

After the talking was over and most of the audience had gone their several ways, a tall, craggy man with prematurely white hair and striking blue eyes approached me. He wanted to offer, he said, "not point-counterpoint, but" his truth, which was the hard-earned kind. When he told me he had been incarcerated in varying degrees of security for "a lot of years," I was taken aback. Here was a teacher.

"I never hurt anybody," he said; "I just kept running away." He was reticent but told his story with urgency. He described the sterile, nightmarish prisons, the perverse logic of ever-stricter punishment, and the mental cruelty of some of the sanctions he'd been subjected to, such as being forbidden to talk with anyone. Clearly, the real horror of imprisonment is the utter antipathy to life, to anything uncontrolled, in those stark penitentiaries.

Finally, the blue-eyed man said, he'd regained his freedom. To rehabilitate himself, he took to the High Sierra. He hiked and hiked and, he said, let nature "straighten him out." What he wanted to impress on me was that Life had sustained and redeemed his life. Even the commonest embodiment of wildness—a jay, a house sparrow, a dandelion—might be some captive soul's only tie to the larger world of free nature.

The tale and the teller were one fierce teaching that nature heals and transforms, that in wildness, as Thoreau declared, is the preservation of the world. Prison, the quintessential

human-made milieu, strives for security and conduces to para-
noia; the prisoning mentality pervades our institutions. To be
limited only to human example and human companionship,
locked up in buildings, and entirely regimented would be a
death in life.

Inhabiting this place of mine, enjoying a woodsy privacy
where, rather than being the prevalent species, human beings
are in a minority of one, has feasted and filled my soul as surely
as trekking John Muir's "range of light" had the soul of that
pilgrim prisoner. This place, mind you, is not the Serengeti
Plain or the Sierra Nevada; it's just some wooded acres that
provide cover for deer, coyotes, porcupines, woodchucks, raccoons, rabbits, squirrels, mice, voles, shrews, snakes, slugs,
toads, frogs, about two dozen bird species, and a near-infinity
of insects and arachnids. It's a woodburban experience, but
being domiciled amid these other lives gives me glimpses of
their wildness and keeps me whole.

An assortment of spiders occupies every corner, angle, and
unvisited space in the house. The pines are always busy with
chickadees and nuthatches darting around, with red squirrels
traveling the boughs. To look out a window and see a maze of
branches, needles, and leaves, to hear chirps and chips and
trills, or simply to watch the soft movement of the cat's breathing as she sleeps, reassures me that there are still galaxies of
lives and destinies here on earth, a vast range of possible ways
to be alive.

In his book *The Day Before America,* a fine and thoughtful
portrayal of the changing natural history of North America
from the last glaciation to the present time, William
MacLeish draws artfully upon the knowledge of both scientists and first peoples. Respectful of the aboriginal ways of life
on this continent, MacLeish perspicaciously characterizes the

ethos of first peoples throughout the Americas as extending "animacy, sentience, and volition" to all beings. It's a useful formulation.

The animacy, sentience, and volition of the life around me are undeniable. The attainments of all these Others, such as finding sustenance deep in the sandy soil, standing patiently through hard winters, burrowing purposefully through the dark earth, soaring and perching, or slithering with nary a rustle through the dry leaves, can only command respect: Everything in nature is alive, is aware, and has a will. These lives have intrinsic meaning. The hornets, phoebes, hummingbirds, and locust trees have no need of my sentiments. Inadvertently, generously, they engross me in life. Their wordless teaching directly addresses the life force in me, avowing it, too, to be good.

Lest my rhapsodizing transport me beyond the perimeters of truth, it behooves me to confess my bigotry toward certain members of the animate, sentient, and volitional crowd. Among these would be the alien invasives of this locale, such as knapweed, autumn olive, and honeysuckle; the burgeoning hordes of adaptive natives, such as ring-billed and herring gulls; and midnight drivers of noisy, big-engined trucks with National Rifle Association decals in the windows and "Choose Life" stickers on the bumpers. For me, the hard-to-love cases are not the leeches, slugs, rats, or cockroaches; they are the human beings who treat nature as a nonentity.

Living alone, I am seldom lonely. Unless I happen to be on the road, traveling to lecture or to attend a conference, or going to a meeting in town, my society consists of plants and animals. I try to keep a household hospitable to life and, within reason, to befriend the Others who share this place with me.

In May 1998, I noticed that a gray tree frog (*Hyla versicolor*), about as big as my thumbnail, was spending its days on a windowsill on the north side of my house. I didn't want to make a pet of this hyla, but I did want to make it welcome. So the frog might have a wet place in a region that was suffering a terribly dry year, I put a little bowl of water with a rock in it on the sill. The frog then kept to itself in the nook between bowl and window. Just its head appeared watchfully over the bowl's rim. The pale tissue of its gullet pulsated frantically while the horizontal irises of its big golden eyes were sleepily closed, giving it a self-contradictory appearance.

Wanting to learn something about my visitor's natural history, I headed for the library. The most enjoyable reference I found was *The Calls of Frogs and Toads*, an audiotape. I began to play the cassettes on my car's tape deck. For a couple of weeks, my drives to town were enlivened by the voices of southern leopard frogs in Mississippi, pig frogs in Florida, American toads in upper New York State, and, of course, the gray tree frog, along with a few dozen other species. Many of these frog and toad calls had been recorded in the field by Lang Elliot, who also narrated the tape. Mr. Elliot, with his own dulcet voice, is a batrachian vocal music fan whose passion for frog-song would make a human diva weep with envy. Out there in the soggy places, Lang Elliot was hearing the amphibian equivalents of Verdi, Wagner, and Mozart choruses and carting sound equipment all over the country to immortalize them. Although the hyla stayed on the sill for a few weeks, I never actually heard or saw it call, and before long I learned the reason why.

My frog-watching was only sporadic, not the dogged gumshoe-on-a-stakeout surveillance that real wildlife biology demands. For instance, returning home after dark one night, I found the frog behaving as one of the frog books said it might. It was clinging to the window glass with a hunter's equipoise, supremely alert to the possibility of catching some of the insects drawn to the porch light nearby. "Oh-ho," methought, "the perfect opportunity to do some nature observation amid all the comforts of home." In I went and raised the shade on the inside of the frog's window, grabbed a snack, pulled up a chair, and settled in. This is the kind of thing that people without television sets do.

The frog's skin was so translucent, I could see the shadow of its bowel within its belly. Because the frog's throat lacked a dark little fold that would indicate a vocal sac, I concluded that my guest was female. Only males call to attract mates. As a field guide had promised, the frog's loins were splashed with saffron flash colors. It is thought that when the frog leaps, the sudden appearance of bright hues startles predators and buys flight time. Her front and hind feet, so delicate and opal, terminated in perfect little toe-pads.

I sat and observed the frog for what I thought was quite a while. For a long time, nothing happened. Nothing happened. Period. The frog clung to the pane. Some lacewings and moths wandered on the glass but didn't interest her. I ran out of the patience essential to catching a glimpse of wildlife action. Ennuied, I headed for bed, wishing the frog *bon appétit*. Another night, there was some excitement. The hyla, hunting, leapt from sill to frame.

This *Hyla versicolor*'s appearance varied not just in color, which was quite changeable, but also in carriage. Sometimes she looked slack, dumpy, and sleepy. Sometimes her skin was a pebbly lichen green; at other times, a nondescript dun. The night of the leap, her eyes were huge and brilliant, shiny brasses, her body taut. Several times a day I peeked at her and topped up the water bowl as necessary. Perhaps the frog thought there was a mountain that loomed periodically to issue a flood of freshwater into her three-inch china pond. She was seldom in plain sight. Her wisdom was in her wariness.

I had to wonder how and why this frog had got to my place, so far from any permanent wetness. The recently vanished ponds in the south center of this section were half a mile away. The tiny lake in the section to the north, epicenter of the spring peeper and chorus-frog din in early spring, is at least that distant and lies across a moderately traveled paved road. Wherever this hyla originated, it was a continent away for someone an inch and a half long. The *Hyla versicolor* can produce its own antifreeze in order to pass through winter's bitterest cold frozen as it slumbers in some duffy little tree cranny. Was this hyla metamorphosed just this year, or had she been through the winter?

She stayed through the better part of that desiccated month of May. Then the rain came. When it did, I happened to remember that the year before, snow had fallen just about that very day. The inconstancy of our weather is a point of local pride. "If you don't like the weather," we say, "just wait a minute."

The rainstorms continued for a few days, boisterously. The slaking they brought was still desperately needed. Thunder and driving rain raised a tumult one night, when I was awakened by lightning at three o'clock in the morning and the ruckus of rain on the roof. It all must have sounded the call of the wild to the hyla.

Would the rain and flowing wetness of every surface prompt the little frog to leap toward likelier surroundings, something more tree-like? The churning, spawning clasp of amplexus—sex—was perhaps but a memory now, tree frogs most likely having mated earlier, as soon as the nights had grown warm. Was she content in her splendid isolation, or was she drawn to moister climes and batrachian society?

The following day, as I was on my way out to do an errand, I visited the frog and moved the little dish to get a good look at her. She stayed put for the minute she was out in the open. As I backed the car out of the driveway, I kept my eye on the hyla. She sat unmoving, a tiny spot of grayish woody color on the cedar-stained sill, a minuscule being distinct against the vastness of house and trees and woodpile. I could see her because I knew where to look. Later in the day, the frog was gone. She never returned to that spot. She might have been someplace close by, seeing me, but it would have taken some luck for me to be able to discern her body, with its perfect camouflage, against the ground, variegated with needles, bark, and lichen, or against the trunks of the trees or in the wrack of light and shadow of the woodpile. Did she travel a furlong? Did she travel a mile? Did she become someone's dinner or the mother of multitudes?

Given the diverse raiment life sports, one never knows what the guises of the gods may be. In more than one culture, frogs have been worshiped. How would the world look today if our species had never ceased to revere and offer libations to the Others?

Metamorphosis is among the most astonishing feats of amphibians and many insects. Creatures that undergo complete metamorphosis live, in one lifetime, two different lives in two different bodies. Changing form to take advantage of different milieus favorable to different phases of life is an old, old strategy. *Amphibian*, in fact, means "double life." Frogs, toads, newts, and salamanders all undergo complete metamorphoses. These pioneering terrestrial vertebrates, whose ancestors appeared before the time of the dinosaurs, have outlasted countless other creatures in the epochs since, but they may not survive us.

Whether or not amphibians live in or near water as adults—and gray tree frogs like my visitor don't—there must be ponds or ephemeral springtime puddles to accommodate mating, egg laying, the development of larvae within the eggs, and the hatching and maturation of the tadpoles and polliwogs in their metamorphosis from aquatic to terrestrial animals. Water is the medium for this astonishing bodily transformation from gills to lungs, from swimming to hopping or leaping, from vegetarian to carnivore. Frogs and toads must gather at the water as soon as they and it are thawed and moving again, or there will be no further generations of their kind. This is one of the many reasons why wetlands preservation and restoration is so urgent. As swamps, creeks, backwaters, marshes, sloughs, and ponds dry up in droughts or are converted to real estate, amphibian populations—indeed, all freshwater-loving creatures—are increasingly threatened.

During evolutionary time, metamorphosis and amphibianism emerged as life patterns that allowed some animals to have a turn in each of two worlds. When those worlds take a turn for the worse, that pattern becomes doubly hazardous. Today, numerous amphibian species all over the planet are in decline or have gone extinct. There is no single cause of these losses. The common condition is amphibian vulnerability to the effects of environmental degradation in the water—pollution and increased predation or disease—and on the land—increased ultraviolet radiation, ever more pavement and therefore frog-squashing traffic, and countless other forms of habitat destruction and disturbance. Amphibians, with their extraordinarily permeable skins, are disastrously exposed to the toxicity of industrial civilization.

In 1991, after a global scientific task force was organized

by the International Union for the Conservation of Nature (IUCN—The World Conservation Union) to investigate the phenomenon, worldwide amphibian decline officially became an issue. The reality of what the vanishing of toads and frogs would mean to my life began to impinge a few years later during a weeklong springtime retreat. I was tucked away in a hermitage on a pond in the vicinity of Kalamazoo, Michigan. At night, after I retired, I lay in the darkness listening to the spring peepers and other batrachians down at the pond. Mentally editing out the noise of the hut's little refrigerator, I concentrated on their antiphony. I tried to distinguish among the voices, to guess how many frogs of how many kinds were calling down at that dwindling, duckweed-choked pond. Place is powerful. Some frog species have regional dialects.

During this close listening, there came to me an image of the glistening, pale interior of the tiny frog's throat, stretched to translucence when calling. I thought of our vertebrate kinship, of my own throat and its voice, and then of my own five-foot-eight, 160-pound body. How much is that in peeper equivalents?

How many ounces of frogs does it take to make a night resound? A mastering energy produces those peeps, trills, and croaks. The calling is about procreation, but amplexus can't be the whole story. Why should we presume that frogs don't take pleasure in the singing itself, in the conviviality of call and response? And what if all those lives become untenable? What if spring nights go mute? Amphibian decline should strike us as evidence of moral calamity. Our species is now in a position akin to that of the drunk driver who kills a family in a hit-and-run accident and then has to take sober responsibility for the slaughter.

There are always less harmful ways to live. The Jains of India are so committed to ahimsa, total nonviolence, that they sweep the sidewalks before them as they walk so as not to tread on any living beings. Jain monks wear breathing masks and strain their beverages for the same reason, as a highly symbolic demonstration of reverence for even the tiniest of lives. Out of respect for frogs, I may desist from eating frog legs, dig a pond in my backyard, refrain from employing poisons for any purpose, and perhaps write to the United States Congress to uphold protection for endangered species, most of which is just sweeping my own personal path.

To avert this moral calamity will require a change in political will—and in our way of life. It is our widely envied consumerism, with its "better living through chemistry," growing numbers of adherents, automotive addiction, and sprawling settlements, that threatens so many other, more venerable ways of being. No crash research and development program is necessary, just a move to adopt the considerable array of alternative technologies, land-use patterns, and mores already available. Could some cultural sobriety and material simplicity follow the recognition that without such change, springtime, amphibian choruses, and countless other manifestations of life's creativity really could fall silent, as Rachel Carson warned?

For me to afford some hospitality to these Others could, like the Jains' sweeping and sieving, come under the heading of religious duty. As the woods all around me are logged, fields are mowed and plowed, orchards are sprayed, and subdivisions encroach, merely by leaving my thirty-five scraggly acres of vegetation undisturbed I'm providing a refuge. By keeping the land taxes paid, may I accumulate merit! Lives are unfolding out back.

There are so many lives in which to find interest, especially during warm weather, when the air fairly teems with moths, bugs, butterflies, flies, beetles, mosquitoes, ants, dragonflies, grasshoppers, bees, skippers, and wasps. There is a great coming forth and flourishing of the six-leggeds, with all their strange talents and beauties. The air hosts creatures buzzing, diving, hithering and thithering, motes in the light, meals for the many.

Insects get a bum rap. Indoors, their presence is taken as an index of filth. Outdoors, they're the enemy, chewing, sucking, boring, girdling, swaddling, undermining, and denuding the gardeners' and farmers' best efforts. Insect plagues are no joke, especially in single-crop agriculture. But insect infestations are more an effect of mispractice and environmental stress than the first cause of crop or forest damage. Like most predators, insects take advantage of the weak or maladapted and the superabundant, the easy marks. In the vast monocultural plantations agribusiness promotes, various insects find uninterrupted expanses of their favorite foods. Because insect generations are many and frequent, evolution helps them stay a jump ahead of chemical and even genetically modified pest controls by favoring the genes of individuals that happen to possess some resistance to the effects of the controls.

Chances are, insects are here to stay. Learn to love 'em or leave the planet. Perhaps I've become captivated by insects because no matter how devastating human actions prove to be finally, members of the class Insecta will abide, and in greater numbers and variety than, say, subphylum Vertebrata. It's an old ratio. They're smaller, commoner creatures, animals whose natural history won't culminate in extinction anytime soon and break my biotic heart. Given the habitat-destroying tendencies that accelerated so wildly during the twentieth century and that show no sign of slowing in the twenty-first, we specimens of *Homo sapiens* interested in wildlife may be left mainly with insects to observe. This is not to say that there aren't endangered insect and arachnid species, but overall, the arthropod approach may prove more enduring than the big, wide-ranging omnivore notion. A famous quip by biologist J. B. S. Haldane speaks to this. When asked what he could tell about God from his studies of nature, Haldane replied that God evidenced "an inordinate fondness for beetles."

Because I'm now both farsighted and nearsighted, my focus is sharpest about seven inches from my eyes. This is an optimum distance for bug watching. So my dilettante entomology is also a function of aging. The smoky-veined mullions of a paper wasp's wing, the bird-poop camouflage of the red-spotted purple butterfly's larva, even the delicate hypodermic mouthparts of the mosquitoes who keen throughout our summers, are, at close range, wondrously beautiful.

The exuberance of fantastic millions of creatures engaged in courtship, predation, migration, metamorphosis, architecture, sociality, and care of the young is all happening right there at the edge of human sight—assuming that the humans doing the seeing have left the insects some habitat and held off with the pesticides. Insects, many but not all of which undergo metamorphosis, have been on earth for 350 million years. Members of the order Lepidoptera, whose transformations from lowly larval caterpillars to delicate aeronauts, whose scaly wings, colorful as flower petals, carry them lilting and gliding through the warm times, are among nature's showiest sleights. They've been doing that trick for between 50 million and 100 million years now.

In insect, as in amphibian, metamorphosis, dramatically different larval and adult bodies allow individual insects to exploit different elements of their environment for different purposes in the course of a single life. One phase is primarily for eating, the other for mating. Lepidopterans first hatch and then go crawling off on an assortment of legs and prolegs to chew plants, books, or clothes. In their larval stages, many lepidopterans are aesthetically challenging. It takes determination and nerves of steel to perceive the beauty of a tomato hornworm, for instance. After the larvae have eaten their fill, they dissolve themselves and pupate. A time passes. The hornworm turns, and presto-change-o: a sturdy, handsome sphinx moth—just one of the 11,000 species of butterflies and moths in North America—emerges and, on the mottled gray wings that were inherent in the larva, goes buzzing off to sip nectar of an evening.

It was several years ago, when I noticed a fuzzy, undulating phalanx of milkweed tussock-moth caterpillars stripping leaf after leaf from the milkweed plants around the house, that I started paying attention to insects. During the day, these hairy, tufted, black, white, and umber caterpillars were devouring what is the monarch butterfly larvae's essential foodstuff. Showing species prejudice, I thought I'd try to favor monarchs over milkweed tussock moths by routing the fuzzy-wuzzies with a blast from the garden hose. Afterward, it dawned on me that my intervention might just have dispersed the tussock-moth caterpillars more widely, washing them into new worlds to conquer.

My next act of monarch chauvinism was to give four monarch caterpillars a lift to a nice, fresh, leafy milkweed. They had pretty well denuded the plant where I found them. The new salad bar elicited no gratifying, mouthpart-smacking enthusiasm. I sat on my haunches for half an hour and watched the elegantly striped monarch caterpillars uncurl from their fright and wiggle their filaments. The next morning, there were four monarch caterpillars placidly grazing in that general neck of the milkweeds, but there was no telling whether they were my protégés. By the following day, all but one caterpillar had disappeared—to greener milkweed or successful metamorphosis?

Apropos this butterfly aid mission, I remembered a teaching story that was a staple of the late David Brower's wisdom.

He recounts it thus in his testament *Let the Mountains Talk,
Let the Rivers Run:*

> In nature, making the wind blow can be a mistake. I know
> because I tried it.
>
> When I was 11, I had the idea of raising butterflies. I
> liked Western swallowtails, which are exquisite creatures
> about three inches in wingspan, yellow with a black bor-
> der. Just above the tail, they have eyespots of a rainbow
> hue. My neighborhood had many swallowtails and was full
> of anise—ample butterfly food. I started with the eggs.
> Tiny caterpillars emerged, yellow-banded squibs of black.
> The caterpillars later turned green and then into
> chrysalides. I waited.
>
> When the day came, the first chrysalis cracked. An
> antenna popped out, another, then the butterfly labori-
> ously climbed out. The abdomen was extended, full of
> fluid that was pumped into the unexpanded wings as the
> butterfly clung upside-down on a twig. Thirty minutes
> later, the former caterpillar was aloft, a miracle—which
> was about to be short-circuited in my desire to help what
> I did not understand.
>
> As the remaining chrysalides split, I lent a finger. Very
> gently, I widened their cracking skins. The creatures
> promptly emerged. They just crawled about. What had
> been genetically designed had been undone. What was
> supposed to happen now could not. The flow of fluid was
> not triggered by the butterfly's own exertions and failed to
> reach the wings. They all died. I had tried to free them,
> and by freeing them I had killed them.

Monarch butterflies are ubiquitous, conspicuous, and
familiar, a perfect subject for the sedentary, netless lepidopter-
ist. On another summer day, I was basking on my back porch
and observing a newly emerged monarch butterfly, wet and
fat-bellied as though just birthed. This time, with precaution
not to help that which I don't understand, I simply watched
the butterfly's work of stiffening its wings for flight. The

empty chrysalis and the butterfly both dangled from the stem of a goat's beard plant right next to the path to my writing studio. Although I travel that path many times a day, I had somehow managed not to see this chrysalis.

The brand-new butterfly in its orange, black, and white regalia clung to the plant, swaying with the breezes of the partly cloudy day. The temperature fluctuated minute by minute from sultry to slightly cool. For a few seconds, a precise shaft of light fell upon the monarch, glorious in its own personal sunbeam. Simone the cat was out with me taking the morning air. She nosed tentatively through the grass and weeds, discovered the butterfly, and gave it a sniff. Simone's inquiry apparently stimulated the monarch to flex its wings once, but there was no way it could have flown from her. I ushered the cat away from the monarch's work in progress and resumed my watch, shifting my observation post to a shadier spot on the ground under a cherry tree. Immediately I was bitten in a sensitive place by some pismire indignant about being sat upon.

From my new vantage point, I spotted a monarch caterpillar just beginning the metamorphosis the other was concluding. Dangling head-down from a piece of siding on the house, the caterpillar shed its skin like a fleshy lady ooching out of her panty hose. Pupating looked arduous, with much writhing required. A few feet away, meanwhile, the newly sprung butterfly was leisurely dangling in the zephyrs, stretching its proboscis. Moments later, the caterpillar, without benefit of limbs or digits, had managed to heave itself entirely out of its clinging skin and gather itself into itself. In a quick reverse-Houdini trick, the butterfly-to-be had encapsulated itself in a glistening celadon ithyphallic form, studded with gold and subtle reliefs portending wings and abdominal segments. Directly beneath the chrysalis lay the cast-off skin, collapsed like a concertina but still possessing the emptied forms of larval eyes and prolegs, filaments and mandibles, the discarded garment of a former life.

The following spring, I had the opportunity to visit one of the monarch butterfly reserves in the mountains of Mexico's transverse neovolcanic belt. Standing in the presence of millions of monarchs, I wondered whether the two sojourners in my backyard were among this lucky multitude that had made the autumn migration and survived the winter.

The monarch is unique among the butterflies in its migration pattern. Near the autumnal equinox, the eastern population, a considerable portion of the world's monarchs, flies, or dies trying, from the northernmost reaches of its territory in southern Canada, New England, and the upper Midwest to a small winter range, perhaps a couple of hundred square miles of forested sky islands, in the mountains of Michoacán State in central Mexico. Monarch populations west of the Rocky Mountains winter in the vicinity of Monterey Bay in California.

By this flight of many hundreds of miles, the late-summer generation of eastern monarchs arrives at a place that for millennia has afforded the specific conditions the butterflies need to live in a torpid state through the winter, conserving the fat reserves they accumulate while nectaring in the fields, meadows, and road margins of Texas and northern Mexico, for a vernal mating orgy.

The climate in these central Mexican massifs is warm enough and the montane *oyamel* forest canopy was, until recent excessive logging, protective enough that the monarchs, clinging by the thousands to cypress and *oyamel* fir-tree trunks and branches, were largely protected from occasional freezing temperatures, snow, and ice. The butterflies could just hibernate. They didn't need to forage except for the occasional taste of water on a warmer day. After mating, the fertilized females, carrying the makings of a new generation, fly northward to the first landfall with milkweed in the southern United States, where they lay their eggs and die. Reproductively active monarchs have brief existences, lasting only from two weeks to a ripe old age of two and a half months. Two or three successive generations, or broods, of butterflies are required to complete the species' full migration. It is the great-grandchildren of those monarchs that flew north in the spring who fly back to Mexico in the fall to repeat the cycle.

Milkweed is sine qua non to the monarch's lifeway, its essential host plant. The caterpillar's milkweed munching is the means by which it concentrates in its body, and thus in the winged butterfly body to come, the plant's cardiac glycosides, distasteful and powerfully emetic chemicals. Once a bird has had a bite of monarch and barfed up its supper, it remains wary of showy orange, black, and white butterflies for the rest of its life. It is by virtue of being repellant to most birds that monarch butterflies can safely gather by the millions in the winter without serving as a bonanza to predators. Viceroy butterflies, which mimic the monarchs but aren't milkweed eaters and thus are not emetic, also enjoy the avian détente negotiated by evolution for the monarch. This is a lifeway of stunning complexity, contingency, beauty, and vast dimension in space, time, and form.

One of Latin America's great men of letters, Homero Aridjis, has by his poetry and ecological advocacy given voice to the rights of nature. Aridjis, who now resides in Mexico City, was born and raised in the village of Contepec, near one of the several monarch colonies. The resplendent butterflies arriving in the mountains around All Souls' Day, drifting up

the village streets in gathering numbers and making their way
to the shelter of the *oyamel* forests higher up in the mountains,
were what first aroused the poet's sensitivity to nature. Aridjis
has had a lifelong affinity for monarchs and has worked dili-
gently to persuade the Mexican government to protect the
monarchs' wintering places. In an interview with Alex
Shoumatoff for a report on the monarchs published in *Vanity
Fair* in 1999, Aridjis recalled: "The hill and the butterflies
faced the village, and as a child I used to go see them. For me,
they are visual music, the apotheosis of light, motion and
beauty, a solar-light symphony. . . . I learned to love nature
through the butterflies."

It was to honor Señor Aridjis' contributions to both literature and the cause of ecology that the Orion Society—a non-
governmental organization based in the United States that,
through its publications and other programs, works to recon-
nect the dominant culture with the natural world—held the
colloquium that in February 2000 brought me and another
dozen nature writers, journalists, poets, activists, and scientists
to the mountains of Michoacán.

The Orion Society colloquium included field trips to
monarch reserves near the city of Zitácuaro, where we stayed.
Among our company were the lepidopterists Lincoln Brower
and Robert Michael Pyle. Brower, now the leading authority
on monarchs, has researched the monarch's metabolism and
migration and puzzled out many of the mysteries of its natural history. He has also become a partner with Homero Aridjis and other conservationists in Mexico and around the world
in an effort to protect the montane forests in the butterfly
reserves. Pyle is a literary man, author of several entrancing
works of natural history in addition to his scientific contributions and his work in invertebrate conservation.

On our arrival at the Sierra Chincua butterfly reserve, we

encountered a roughshod version of ecotourism. The reserve is part of an *ejido,* a communal landholding. For almost a century, the *ejidatarios* have been deriving their subsistence from their land, using and selling the timber, pasturing animals in the forests, and over time expanding their lowland corn cultivation farther and farther up the volcanic slopes. The *ejidatarios,* nominally banned from logging by a 1986 presidential decree establishing several such sites as butterfly reserves, are hoping to profit instead from visitation to their land. Their livelihood must come from the land somehow, and as free trade levels the planet, rural subsistence has been subordinated to the demands of the world market. As Peter Sauer wrote in *Orion* magazine in spring 2001, "What is killing the monarch is the U.S. economy. The force that drives the globalization of agriculture and international trade on this continent is U.S. consumerism."

Visitation is definitely the term to describe what went on at the Sierra Chincua reserve. Parking in the high meadow near the trailhead where we would set out on our trek to the monarch colonies was random. Of sanitary facilities there were none, making for stench in the thickets. There was an aggregation of stalls constructed of slab wood, perhaps two dozen cobbled-together bodegas, cafés, soda fountains, and souvenir shops. Among the souvenirs were toy logging trucks.

We had been warned that the journey to the monarchs would be strenuous, with lots of climbing and descent, all at about 10,000 feet, which altitude itself can challenge the cardiovascular system; however, we'd also been advised that horses could be hired. I thought I could travel by shank's mare, and I hiked perhaps 100 yards on the strength of my conviction. Five minutes into the initial climb, I felt as though my heart were bursting—indeed, as if it would erupt from my bosom and flop, fibrillating, by the trailside—not from nature epiphany but from exertion. And so, for some part of 150 pesos—about ten U.S. dollars—an eleven- or twelve-year-old wrangler named José rented me a tough little pony and led the horse by its halter to, and then from, the footpath that was the last stretch of the way to the densest aggregations of butterflies.

Afterward, many of us would liken our trip to a pilgrimage. The steady stream of people on the trail consisted by and large of Mexicans, folks of all ages, numerous grandmothers trudging stately and determined among them. When we reached the meadows where we were to dismount and walk, the query "How much farther to the butterflies?" was heard, as it would be with increasing frequency for the next forty-five minutes. The trail was warm and suffocatingly dusty, steep and knee-challenging, crowded, and physically taxing. We hiked down to the forest grove, where the monarchs had gathered the year before. As we walked, I saw more and more butterflies, more than I had ever seen in my life, but still no solid colonies. The butterflies, following ever-scarcer water, had set up camp farther downslope this year than last.

A little more trekking and we beheld them: tens of millions of monarchs weighing down the cypress and fir branches, blanketing the tree trunks, glittering in the sunlit openings, floating like flakes of gold and amber in the lapis sky. It was a wonder outstripping language. The butterflies were so numerous that they painted the grove orange, so numerous that their millions of wings together stirring in the warmth made a soft, breezy sound. It was a transcendent experience, yet it brought to mind Oscar Wilde's observation that "each man kills the thing he loves."

Every last visitor, pony wrangler, plant, and butterfly

within the vicinity of the continually expanding braid of trails was coated with and choking on a fine coat of volcanic soil pulverized to dust by the passage of *zapatos*, Vibram soles, hooves, and tires. The damage to these mountainsides by the helter-skelter trailblazing of adoring hikers, ponies carrying nonhikers, and trucks carrying still more nonhikers was severe. Add to that the persistence of logging, both legal and outlaw, of the *oyamel* forest, the Achilles' heel of the eastern monarchs, and Lincoln Brower estimated that if nothing were to change, the monarch butterflies would have perhaps five more years. In addition to these threats to their wintering grounds, the monarchs are threatened by agricultural practices in the U.S. corn belt, which overlaps the breeding range of about half their population. Here, the threats come from herbicides used to rid the fields of "noneconomic" plants such as milkweed and from the windblown pollen of corn genetically engineered to kill the larvae of lepidopteran crop pests. Monarch caterpillars ingesting corn pollen that has drifted onto milkweed leaves suffer "collateral damage."

In an article about Aridjis published in the *Amicus Journal* in 1998, Dick Russell, who was a member of the Orion Society colloquium, wrote:

> During the years in the 1960s and 1970s that he lived abroad as a diplomat and teacher, Aridjis would make an annual winter pilgrimage back to his hill. As the trees were cut for firewood, the presence of the butterflies diminished. "I felt that my own childhood was being killed, my memory of a natural beauty that had once overwhelmed me," Aridjis recalls. "The possibility of my village becoming a wasteland, a silent country without wind in the trees or animal sounds or birdsongs, made me feel desperate. Butterflies became for me a symbol of life's fragility."

Everywhere on earth, it seems, it is our species that needs to transform itself: to become as different from what we are now as the butterfly is from the leaf-chewing caterpillar, as different as the milkweed fluff is from the starry flowers whose nectar feasts the paper-thin airborne monarchs.

5

SUMMER

Growing up in the Valley of the Sun, where summer temperatures were in the triple digits, I had no idea how lush and enthralling a season summer could be. In Phoenix, summer was fun because school was out and my cronies and I could join forces in beating the heat. One year we regaled ourselves by hauling in 100 pounds of block ice from a plant on the other side of town to cool our backyard swimming pool as though it were a drink. In the San Francisco Bay Area, there wasn't any summer as such. Powerful summer heat inland, east of the coastal hills, drew fog through the Golden Gate, making San Francisco a gray and chilly place, especially of an evening.

Thus, my first experience of an early July in the upper Midwest, with warm, bare-arm nights, burgeoning green woods and woodlots, shimmering fields of hay, ruby-jeweled cherry orchards, an azure Great Lake, emerald inland lakes, and bright, sandy beaches, captivated me for good and all. The fact that I was cruising around the county with my good-looking, dashing, and goofy ex-husband-to-be in Rob's vintage red convertible compounded my interest exponentially. Many popular songs began to make more sense.

As it happened, I arrived in this land of summer's epitome about the time the greenhouse effect began changing summer's warmth from pleasure to menace. The decade of the 1980s was the hottest on record—until the record-breaking 1990s came along. Of late, our summers have brought more heat and less rain, lower lake levels, and, despite all that, still more tourists.

For the time being, though, simplicity is perhaps at its most epicurean around the summer solstice. Picnicking becomes a real possibility, and here the refreshment of swimming is handy by.

Although it was ordinary enough when my parents were young, it's become a rare thing to be able to take a dip in a clean, scenic swimming hole that's a part of the commons. In this woodsy glacial landscape, however, it's less rare than anywhere else I've been. As the amenities that are actually necessities grow ever scarcer, the human psyche frays and the fabric of community life is rent. An archaic liberty such as the freedom to go for a swim, entrusting yourself to yourself, is a shaping kind of freedom, a kind of liberty critical to developing and sustaining one's strength of person. To be fully present in the body and in the body of nature is an old, old need.

Although I'm only a middling swimmer, slow but dogged, self-taught and imperfectly hydrodynamic, I'm about the only person around here who uses our neighborhood lake for distance swimming, so there's one small pond in which I'm peerless. On summer weekends, the children and occasional parents entering this lake keep to the shallow water and generally hug the shore. The fact that I sometimes swim the length of the lake and back, a distance of less than a mile, may excite comment, which in turn excites my pride.

I know I'm setting the kids a bad example by swimming alone. Well-meaning friends, neighbors, and strangers have scolded me for this foolhardiness. They figure I'm risking not only drowning but also foul play. I consider my swims, whether solitary or in the pool, to be the premiums on my health insurance. I don't think I'm overconfident. For thirty years now, I have been swimming for exercise and pleasure. For two of those years, I was swimming many a morning in the waters of San Francisco Bay, albeit as a member of a club. Those bay swims were always cold and often rough.

By late June, no later than July, the inland lakes around here, including that neighborhood lake, a nonpareil swimming hole right nearby, have warmed up enough that going for a swim under the open sky instead of driving the fifteen miles to the Boardman City civic center pool to do some chlorinated laps becomes the obvious choice.

When I made my first fateful visit to the county, the swimming hole was the first place Phil took me on that Fourth of July fling that got parlayed into a whole new existence. After a four-hour flight from San Francisco and the drive out from the airport, we went swimming by starlight in this paradisaical little lake. There was one lone cottage on the lake's wooded shores back then. Its water-skiing owners paid it an annual weeklong visit. For the rest of the summer, the lake was an obscure little lido for families with kids and their inner tubes, for fishers with low-horsepower boats, and for the occasional swimmer. Being too small for rampant motorized recreation, it's perfect for swimming. A few years after that auto accident that mangled my right leg, the lake became the destination of my first tentative bike rides. Its waters were the medium in which I slowly regained my physical strength. After the divorce, the lake was where I rediscovered the joy in my body.

Once, following a cool, solitary weekday swim under glowering, sprinkly skies, I began wandering the shore on an impromptu litter patrol, collecting snuff tins, bait containers, bottle caps, and assorted wrappers and bits of plastic in a shopping bag I'd brought along. I drew the line at picking up and packing out a soggy, stinky disposable diaper. I'm not that good a Girl Scout. This lakeside cleanup campaign led me off my routine track. I prowled up into the shoreline vegetation and the woods behind it, where, I happily discovered, a good variety of plants grew; some of them, such as marsh skullcap, were new to me. It was the first time in the decade-plus of visiting the lake I had made that landward exploration, and inadvertently at that. Slowly but surely, by virtue of being a part-time homebody, I'm coming to know and understand my vicinity. Every self-propelled outdoor excursion—strolling, swimming, bicycling, or cross-country skiing—is a kind of saga, rich in incident and significant detail—significant to my life, anyway, which is being lived right here.

Since the arrival of residences around the lake, my swims and occasional rambles have ceased to be purely solitary. There may be onlookers unseen in those houses. Although I am put out by the thought that their lawns may be adding pesticides, fertilizers, and sediment to the medium of my swims, I suppose the bright side of the woodburb development around the lake is that now, if I start to founder mid-swim, one of those householders might try to do something helpful, or would at least be able to tell the sheriff to start dragging for my body.

Is it strange to be singing one's death song in the midst of such a vitalizing activity? Well, life and death do seem to be inseparable, a fact that's been vulgarly contorted. As nature is effaced and degraded, so is our understanding of life's cycling, its seamy origins in flesh and earth, in hunt, harvest, and decay. There's such an overriding focus on the human individual that we are desperately aware of lethal intraspecies violence in every setting and at every scale, from the schoolroom to the nation-state. Yet the violence casually done to the Others and to their homes is not perceived as such by most folks. It's okay for everything else to die, but not us human beings.

A few years ago, at the turnoff to the lake, there appeared a billboard advertising narrow lots, pivoting like the sticks of a Japanese fan on a minimal hub of lake frontage; next to it, a cheery sign announced a future subdivision. By and by, the lots began to sell, and each sale was proclaimed by the execrable map. Every time I bicycled past the sign on my way for a swim, I'd damn the developer and his success. After a year of this, I decided that this reflexive hostility was bad for my soul. I'm not exactly sure why, but I called the developer to ask if he would meet with me. I felt a need for a face-to-face encounter with this person I'd demonized, for us to talk as human beings, for him to know what that place meant to me and for me to offer amends for my bad-vibing. I was probably hoping for a miracle. What I got was an encounter that reduced me to tears, which is not all that easy to do. After I had thanked him for agreeing to see me and confessed that I had been angry with him about the development at the lake, he told me about the deed restrictions imposed on the parcels of land, including setbacks, no unsanctioned cutting of trees greater than a certain diameter, and a prohibition of motorized watercraft on the lake. He thought he was doing a good job.

When I told him that I was there because I cared about what happened to all the life around the lake, I'd used up my time. The man flew into a rage. He hotly vented regret that the long-ago owners of the lake had granted any public access to it whatsoever. He rightly pegged me as an environmentalist and an Indian-lover. He more or less suggested that I and my sentimental ilk were bent on snatching the bread from the mouths of his babes, and on and on. About then, I burst into tears, which didn't even break his stride.

The subdivision proceeded, the developer's babes were fed, and several very big houses with garish greenswards sited a respectful distance up-slope from the water's edge now breach the lakeside woodland. Docks and paddleboats belonging to those households mar the shore. There are driveways now, and grassy clearings. The effect of this land-use pattern is the usual: fragmentation of the landscape, reducing its biotic integrity, stability, and beauty. Commonplace suburban conditions—lawns, prowling house cats, septic systems, gaps in the forest canopy, vehicles unpredictably crossing what used to be the nocturnal animals' paths to the water, rank vegetation flourishing in the sunny paths of soil disturbance, noise during the birds' nesting seasons, and additional tykes making a pastime of catching frogs and fish, in competition with the herons—are hard on all but the weediest plants and animals; *sic transit* paradise.

In addition to legions of land speculators, there are other, less systematic despoilers of paradise. Late one early August day, I bicycled over to the lake for a swim. The weather had been moist and balmy, with clouds and breezes, following much-needed rain earlier in the week. After turning off the pavement and pedaling down the shady tunnel of the dirt road, I emerged from the trees and coasted down the gravel hill to the beach. I saw that I was not alone. A glum, shirtless, balding man was hanging out in his parked car. Right beside the lake, just sitting in a truck, were a couple of sunburnt, tattooed longhairs—biker types, I thought. I exchanged minimal greetings, propped my bicycle against a young maple tree, and removed my backpack, helmet, gloves, sneakers, spectacles, and the shorts I had worn over my bathing suit while cycling. I pulled on my bathing cap and walked into the water. The men in the truck were about to leave. Of the water one of them offered, "It's almost too warm."

"It'll do," I returned, and dove in, following my bliss out into the lake. After I'd kicked out a few yards underwater, I bobbed up, doing the breaststroke and freestyle, and then I swam the backstroke and the upside-down breaststroke, an individual medley.

After completing the first leg of the swim, I rested in the water, hands clasped behind my head, legs extended, toes pointed. When I exhaled, my face, elbows, and toes were all that broke the surface. When I inhaled, my chest and belly would bob up, too. For a few minutes I floated, cradled in the cool water, breaching and sinking like a drowsy whale. I would have been perfectly happy to dissolve into the lake, but I made myself swim on across, sometimes pushing myself and sometimes goofing off, loving the weightless, easy exertion, the strong, rhythmic breathing, the syncopated movement of four limbs, neck, and head.

By the time I climbed out of the water, I had the public sliver of shoreline to myself. The truck and the car and their respective occupants were gone. The swim had tuned up my senses, set me on the Beauty Way. The sight of a red dragonfly, exquisite in its pause on the stem of a rush, overwhelmed my vision.

As I dried off and pulled on my shorts and shirt, I mused on another dragonfly hovering near me. I doubt that this interest was mutual. Size-wise, I was clearly out of range of being a mate or a meal. I probably appeared to be an animate snag. I don't take my lack of relevance to dragonflies personally. It's okay with me that sex and hunger make the world go round and that those drives condition our interests, be we dragonflies or draggin' ladies. These good and essential desires prompt what's fundamentally a healthy curiosity in others, an alertness that is piqued from the start by the will to survive. In the quiet the men left behind, the birds were calling and singing, reasserting themselves. I savored the moment and then bicycled home.

On my trip to the lake the next day, following that passing encounter with the glum bald guy and the two men in the truck, I was set on notice that there might be malefactors in this very neighborhood. It was a warm, late-summer Sunday afternoon. Several families with children were enjoying the lake. When I came to a stop and propped my bike against an aspen, a kid piped up, "Daddy, it's that girl who swims." Daddy, a tattooed longhair, was sitting on a beach blanket talking with Mama and having a smoke. Their busy beagle pup was tied to a tree with a sufficiency of leash, provided with a dish of water and a towel for habitat. The family's two or three children were playing in the water. The longhaired father told me that he'd seen me arrive at the lake the day before, and he and his buddy hadn't liked the looks of that other guy who was hanging around. They had waited in their truck for him to leave before they went home. I thanked the man for looking out for me. I felt as though I didn't thank him enough— indeed, couldn't have thanked him enough—but he didn't seem to want to chat, so I headed into the water for a short swim. When I was done, my guardian angel and his family were gone. A different family occupied their spot, a mother watching her blond, curly-headed little boy make repeated forays down to the water and return each time with some new thing for Mama to see, from how wet he'd gotten to how he'd made his toy boat go.

Meanwhile, the implication of the fact that one local perfect stranger had thought it necessary to protect me from another imperfect stranger was sinking in and making my skin crawl. On the one hand, it was a great thing that there had been a Good Samaritan, a gallant man looking out for a woman who, he may well have thought, was too foolish to look out for herself. He'd done a neighborly act of human decency and communal responsibility. When, from the sidelines, I see girls or young women in circumstances that might turn dubious, I, too, try to extend that kind of watchful protection. Nevertheless, it was wretched to remember that by accident of gender and disposition, I'm fair game. Time and again I've repudiated the thought that by going about unescorted, doing things by myself, and living solo in a glass house in the woods, I'm just asking for it. But after a friend who lived by herself in the woods narrowly escaped a knife attack by an unmedicated psychotic stalker, those concerns for my personal safety became harder to dismiss. Hideous things do happen here. But, the inner pep talk goes, I refuse to let testosterone terrorism abrogate my freedom.

That night, remembering the flat animus of the shirtless man's expression when we exchanged hellos, I was afraid in my own home, feeling vulnerable and conspicuous, too easy to follow and find.

Even before I became an object of chivalry, I had come to think of my relation to the lake as like that of a canary to a mine shaft—risky, but not inevitably fatal. Some of those miners' canaries must have died of old age. As the water quality in the lake goes, so may go my health. That water gets into my eyes and gurgles in my ears. I can't keep it from splashing into my nostrils and on down the back of my throat. If I came down with some weird waterborne illness, there would be, in such ailments of my person, evidence suggestive that housing developments degrade the quality of nearby water bodies and the human bodies that swim in them.

Likewise, if I fell victim to foul play, that would indicate a decline in the quality of life here. Random violence is as yet uncommon in the county. Perhaps it's a lack of population density. Here, the custom of neighbors looking out for one another still holds. Neither watersheds nor their human communities fare terribly well, though, in a regime that deals in land, lives, and time as salable commodities. These crude abstractions take their toll. My confidence in my vicinity and the quiet joy I found in active solitude was one casualty, lost to the anger seething in another casualty, a creep lurking on the outskirts of paradise.

It was about ten years ago that I got a bike for my trips to the swimming hole. To drive the car that two and a half miles to the lake to get some exercise was, I realized, both self- and planet-defeating. In our compartmentalized middle-class lifeway, physical fitness has come unrooted from practical capability. There's a stationary bike offered in every garage sale. Evidently the gerbil-wheel version of bicycling is not all that convincing.

The bicycle is a plain machine, the most energy-efficient means of travel available and one that provides much more than transportation. In bicycling, one gains strength and spends time out-of-doors, seeing, hearing, and smelling details that automotive speed blurs to oblivion. The bicycle also provides epicurean pleasure in the form of the pain one's conscience doesn't have for needlessly burning gasoline and churning carbon dioxide into the atmosphere.

Back when I decided to try bicycling, fixing the greenhouse problem wasn't uppermost in my mind. With some serious trauma fresh in my memory, I wasn't confident that I could ride a bike at all, let alone keep at it. Given my doubts, a starter bike seemed like the thing. In Boardman City, there's an old man who runs a secondhand bicycle dealership on his front porch. He sold me a coppery one-speed with coaster brakes for $15. Being a good Luddite and, frankly, technologically challenged, I have no hankering for an abundance of gears. I already have enough opportunity to bollix up a transmission in my car.

A one-speed bike was a good test of my cycling earnestness. For two summers I rode it to the lake for my swims, doing the Tamarack City biathlon. By then, I knew I'd keep on cycling. I thought I might even be ready for a bicycle with a few gears and hand brakes. This time, I went to the sporty cyclist's store in uptown Boardman City to see if I could find myself a slightly more advanced pre-owned model. Fortune smiled, and $40 bought me somebody's castoff customized touring bike, a three-speed with a featherweight silver frame, upright aluminum handlebars, nicely engineered crank-arms, and pedals with toe-clips. The toe-clips took some getting used to after Rob referred to them as suicide baskets.

The bike had racing tires when I purchased it. I rode swiftly, if without much traction or shock absorption, for a year, until I was sure it was true love between me and this bike and could seal the commitment with some customization of my own. The bike was already an individual and had shown a willingness to adapt. Its current circumstances included unpaved roads and an unracy rider. Different tires were called for.

For these, I went to downtown Boardman City and the old-fashioned multipurpose bike shop that deals in everything from training wheels to deluxe derailleurs. There, I could have the bike tuned up, whatever mysteries that entails, and purchase some wider, treadier tires without being cowed by a flippant, lean clientele of riders training for their double centuries.

Miles, the mechanic at the downtown cyclery, proved to be gracious, articulate, intelligent, and a real looker of about my age and height. He admired my bicycle and affirmed that it was ideal for touring, good basic two-wheeled transportation. Miles even intimated that I'd made off with a bargain; the cutting-edge bike dealer who'd sold it must not have recognized what a gem it was.

Chatting with a handsome, helpful bike mechanic was frosting on the cake, so tasty that it prompted a flurry of accessorization. To get a closer look at Miles, I made multiple trips to the bike shop, enhancing my bike with new handgrips, a bell, and generator-powered headlights and tail lights. Before I went for laser-cut streamers to flutter dazzlingly from the handgrips, or a horn, I found out that despite the absence of a wedding ring, Miles was already spoken for, quite contentedly so. He may not be an eligible bachelor, but he remains a renaissance bike mechanic, and our transactions, if a little less frequent than before, continue to be one of the many pleasures bicycling has brought me.

Bicycling also has its dangers. According to John C. Ryan in *Seven Wonders: Everyday Things for a Healthier Planet*, "lacking safe places to bike, bikers face a greater average risk of being killed by a car in each mile on a trip than drivers do." But as my friend Katie Alvord, a transportation activist and author, reassuringly notes in *Divorce Your Car! Ending the Love Affair with the Automobile*, "fewer than two percent of traffic fatalities involve cyclists." Most of those fatalities befall helmetless riders. Out here in the county, we don't have many bike lanes or even paved road shoulders. Like most cyclists, I feel outnumbered and outgunned by the automotive traffic racing by. When I must travel the busier county roads or Boardman City streets, I do so in a kamikaze spirit.

Shortly after I got my starter bike, a fey and gentle man with whom I'd dallied sent me a bicycle helmet rather than flowers as a sayonara gift and persuaded me to be scrupulous about wearing it. My brain is my working capital. If my head were to get remodeled by a sudden meeting with some asphalt, I'd be bankrupt. When I ride, I'm as careful as a daydreamer can be. That's probably not enough. I pedal along with only my helmet and my wits for protection, telling myself that if I should wind up in that unlucky 2 percent of road-killed cyclists, at least I'll have been doing something I liked right up to the very last.

Even before I got my helmet, I had some authentic bicycle gloves with easeful gel padding in the palms. These had been a gift from a friend when I was crutching around. To use crutches properly, you must support your weight on the heels of your hands. My sweet, savvy friend figured that cyclist's gloves might be a help. The fact that for some years now I've been using those gloves for cycling rather than hobbling testifies that nature heals.

The gloves and helmet are the only articles of real bicycling apparel I possess. For the rest, I have arrived at a bicycling costume that is the last word in bargain funk. Spending the cost of a week's groceries on the latest design in athletic footwear would be, in my opinion, crazy. Buying the famous sweatshop brands is dubious, so I wear Dennis-the-Menace-style sneakers. For streamlined helmet-wearing, I braid my hair, and I carry my towel and bathing cap in a day pack. I take a perverse pride in this homely getup, feeling a mite holier than the folks who choose to invest in expensive, enviable sportswear.

I was glorying in my simplicity one day as I set off down the road for a swim. Just at the intersection with the county road, there's a neat little cemetery with old and new headstones, bright plastic bouquets, and medallions indicating that Union Army veterans rest there. This graveyard demands a moment of solemnity before I make the turn onto the busy county road that goes by the lake. This day, as I approached the cemetery, I saw a big silvery blue sedan parked there by the road and experienced a little spasm of self-righteousness for being on a bicycle rather than in a car. A solitary woman sat behind the sedan's wheel. She had taken off her glasses and was wiping her eyes. For a second, my passage distracted her. There was the raw earth of a new grave in the cemetery. Suddenly I felt insolent in the presence of this grief and wished for the woman's consolation; then I turned onto the county road, hoping, as always, not to be hit.

It is a gift to be simple; without compassion, though, it's just pietism. When, in the fullness of my simple life, I chanced to witness tears shed into the empty gape of death, my piety was, and deserved to be, checked.

Even though only a few of the miles I travel are bicycle miles, when I'm using my bike my conscience is a little easier. I make several car trips a week into Boardman City for meetings, grocery shopping, and library visits. I always try to make them multipurpose and to plan my driving route so as not to waste miles. Still, that stop-and-go driving is the most polluting and the most avoidable. In the summer of 2000, I discovered that I could ferry my bicycle into Boardman City with the car and then bike to my various destinations in town on the handy bike trail that allows for safe and entertaining errand-running. It's a fair-weather thing so far. I haven't equipped myself for cycling in rain and snow, but given the funds and some attractive personnel in the sporting goods store, year-round cycling could be next.

Being at least as much eco-puritan as epicurean, I got my bike for transportation, period. Riding it for any purpose, though, usually winds up being fun. That initial investment in the bicycle bought me a synthesis of recreation, transportation, and physical education, all for a pittance.

In contrast, my initial investment in and addiction to my car have brought me complicity in global climate change and the legion of other forms of environmental degradation that automobile manufacture causes. Katie Alvord is living proof that a car is not indispensable to a life like mine. Katie has slipped the greasy toils of automobile ownership completely. Not only has she managed without cars while living in the country, first in northern California and now in the Upper Peninsula of Michigan, she also made the publicity tours for her book *Divorce Your Car!* without resorting to cars or planes. Katie is not suggesting that everyone quit driving cold turkey, just that it is quite possible to make the segue from cars to more lifesome alternatives.

If enough Americans choose bikes over cars for short trips, which most car trips are, and agitate for traffic regulation that favors bicycles and public transportation, we can reduce our monstrous output of smog and greenhouse gases. Eventually, we can undo much land-devouring pavement and sprawl and restore the presence of nature and all its free delights to our settlements.

For the time being, I am trying to be parsimonious about my automobile use and intend to drive my aging compact until its chassis rusts away entirely, leaving a naked engine and drive train. To promote its longevity, I take care of my car. One spring morning, when the car needed some expert attention from the auto mechanic, whose shop is just six miles away, I hauled my bike along to get myself back home. The day before, I had scouted a route that provided a safe and scenic alternative to the frighteningly hectic state highway that goes by the garage. The road home wound for a few miles past dairy farms and orchards and on to a nice flat stretch running by some cornfields and a trout farm. The fruit trees had already blossomed, and the first of many doses of chemicals had been whirled onto the cherries- and apples-to-be. Signs warning of these toxic sprays were posted at the orchards' outskirts. In riding by, I suppose I got a snootful of poison.

Despite the pesticides directed at the fruit trees, there were dancing nebulae of insects at eye level, mayflies maybe, ticking into the straps of my bike helmet as I braked and coasted my way down the curvy two-lane blacktop. I remembered an old joke. Q: How do you spot happy motorcyclists? A: Look for the bug stains on their teeth. Remembering the punch line helped me contain my toothy grin, gleeful as I was to be out on such a bonny day.

Poplar fluff was drifting easily on the air. Crickets were trilling in the grasses. An oriole flashed by. An eastern kingbird, a fearless flycatcher whose appearance ratifies summer, zipped across an intersection. Too often on their insect-hunting sweeps across open spaces, some of which happen to be roads, kingbirds intersect with cars. With bike transportation, there's no roadkill. On a bicycle, it is even possible to avoid collisions with butterflies and grasshoppers.

As I sweatily neared home, I thought about all the well-remunerated people who pay handsomely to go bicycle touring. Although my ride hadn't been an everyday thing but something of a treat, all I'd done was take an hour to do something the long way, to pedal and coast and walk and huff and rest and climb. Would that everyone who wished to do so could have a good life brimming with harmless delights, with activities and occupations that bring health and heightened attention and endless opportunities to exchange greetings with nature!

Compared with car travel, bicycling is an orgy of the senses; so much more sensation envelops the rider and demands attention. The lay of the land, for instance, becomes highly consequential to the question of whether an errand is bikeable or not. From my house to Tamarack City, it's a pleasant four-mile bicycle trip northwest, on mostly quiet roads across amenable, downward-sloping country. Outbound, there's coasting, with the exhilaration of wind in the face, over the low ripple of hills shaped by the glacier's recession; on the fairest days, it's a fest of bright blue skies, puffy white clouds, crystal-clear air, and lively breezes.

With the summer solstice, the year reaches its point of inflection. Here and there, a maple leaf is crimsoned. The apple trees glint with ripely scarlet fruit. The nighttime temperature may dip to the forties a time or two. Days come when the colors are as jewel-like as Gothic altarpieces, when the air is so fresh and good that to breathe is a sacrament. Then, on hot, dry days the grasshoppers come back in force, popping up everywhere. The number of snake fatalities at the road verges seems to rise. Depending on which direction I'm going, some sacramental breathing is heavier than other.

The ride back from Tamarack City takes effort. Homeward bound, I pedal up a gradual incline and then turn off the main road and walk the bike up the sharp slope to the crest of Tower Hill, which at more than 1,000 feet of elevation is one of the highest points in the county. There, I surrender my mass to gravity, which thrillingly whips me down to the stop sign at the intersection. For the rest of the trip home, there's more climbing than coasting, with a penultimate hill that I approach like the Little Engine That Could, saying to myself, "I think I can, I think I can, I think I can."

High summer editions of this trip can feel like a whole lifetime, with all the interplay of fast and slow, of toiling uphill and then hurtling, agreeably terrified, down. Every pebble on the road is palpable. As I pass by dim, cool woods and hot, glaring fields, the quick changes of light and temperature are dizzying. The pungency of alfalfa and manure in the air is overpowering, and the cries of killdeer pierce like the call that will sound on Judgment Day.

One clement Saturday in early October, as fall approached chromatic apogee, helped by nighttime temperatures briefly diving into the thirties, I had an errand in Tamarack City and decided to ride my bike there. The ride outbound was cloudy, cool, and moist. Early fogs were dissipating, the solar disk a circle burning white through a ragged scrim of gray. A few birds were still around, singing, and it may have been a frog I heard peeping in one of the patches of hardwoods interspersed with the fields and house lots I passed. After I'd done my business, I took the high road home. There was a last hurrah of flowers at the pavement's edge: the indefatigable lavender knapweed, pale pink Bouncing Bet, Wedgwood blue chicory, and, by the deeper woods up on Tower Hill, goldenrod and the deep pink flowers of one of the cranesbill tribe. I walked the bike up past an uninhabited but working apple and cherry farm on the west side of the road and the beckoning but gloomy woods to the east.

Somewhere back in those woods, a few years ago, some hunters had finally discovered the remains of a neighbor. He had left a note announcing his intention to commit suicide and to do the deed someplace in the county where he'd never be found. His disappearance was a shock and a loss to the neighborhood. He had been a complex, innovative guy who tried out all kinds of strategies toward land renewal and self-reliance on a small farm in our section. A Vietnam veteran, he had long suffered from, and in the end succumbed to, depression.

The challenge implicit in his suicide note prompted his friends and others to try to find his body. Local outdoorsmen combed the countryside throughout the fall, finding no sign. This raised hopes that he might not have killed himself but simply gone away. Sadly, his corpse lay undiscovered just north of his home for almost a year, with these beeches, maples, hemlocks, and basswoods for his pall.

Knowing that a melancholy, violent deed and its grisly belated conclusion happened here deepens these woods. The trees were the neighbor's last company, undertaker, and graveyard. Memento mori. I noticed a little stand of cranesbill strong along the length of a fallen branch, blossoming late into the year, battening on the wood's dank demise, as I passed by.

I pushed on, gained the top of the hill, and caught a glimpse of Carp Lake off to the east, of the richly colored forested ridges rolling away to Portage Bay. At my feet was the straight, screaming shot down Tower Hill, and then middle-aged me was highballing toward the intersection for a few glorious death-defying seconds with wind pummeling my face, my eyes all around, watching for vehicles coming onto the slope from the side roads that cut through a pine plantation, my baggy turtleneck flapping around my chest, nervous sweat evaporating in the cool, quick air. It was a vast relief to come to a standstill all in one piece at the stop sign.

A subdivided, overspecialized psyche seldom knows plain ecstasy. "By the artificial separation of soul and body," said Oscar Wilde, "men have invented a Realism that is vulgar and an Idealism that is void." All those civilized rifts between mind and body, work and play, getting things done and getting in shape, between living and making a living and even between sacred and mundane, open marketing opportunities. So many pieces of once-whole lives have been separated out and sold back to us as programs, appliances, or religious or professional services that when some of those parts fall back into place of their own accord, there's a spurt of hopeful unity along with the endorphin.

Back at my desk, constrained by a language and semantics imbued with the mind–body dichotomy, I find myself groping

for graceful, accurate ways to tell of the exhilaration that com-
pletes me, that puts the lie to the idea that the mind is local-
ized in the head and that the body is mere apparatus. The
intellect may recognize it, but joy lays claim to the whole
being, and how on this planet could we know joy without
admitting that death is here, too?

It's not that the commonplace ecstasies can't be teased
apart and detailed passionately, but that infinite instant of
wholeness—when the heart sings "Long live the living," when
the mystery is immanent in the jolts to the palms grasping the
handlebars, and in the soil and sunshine turned into trees, and
in the molecules of ammonia wafting out of the cow barn—
trumps thought altogether.

6

CONVIVIALITY

Onions and butter; flour, celery, and salt: all the makings of the soup except for the well water came from the co-op. There were no ingredients that couldn't have been grown here given the right farms, farmers, and markets. Even the dill and caraway seed that flavored it could have been the produce of somebody's garden.

Even in America, even in an information age, food is not something to take for granted but a matter of life and death. It's strange to live in a time that has alienated almost all of us from direct participation in providing our food. It takes good land and a lot of work and skill to produce food well and in salable quantity. For most of us, even the more successful gardeners, the farmer is the woman or man who keeps us fed. I know some of the organic farmers in these parts. They combine entrepreneurial acumen, soil nurturing, plant and animal husbandry, mechanical skill, and fortitude to encourage the land to sustain the people. These are the folks who should be getting the genius grants. My farmer friends, I notice, live in their bodies, articulating their intelligence and creativity physically. They seem less deluded by the culture's departmentalization of physical and mental than anyone else I know.

Hunger, too, unifies and focuses the being. To be able to reply to its demands through the pleasure of cooking has become one of those ancient everyday activities for which few people have the time. There are even prefabricated peanut butter sandwiches for busy schoolchildren. Puttering in the kitchen to make myself a meal, using simple foods, tools, and skills, could be regarded as a luxury in a world where fast food, junk food, or insufficient food are the commoner portion.

Celery is such a polysensory foodstuff, with its unassertive but lingering flavor, with all those strings and all that crunch. After dicing the celery, I chop the onion as quickly as I can and still keep my fingertips, blinking back the tears. Working with onions must be nearly as old as cooking itself. An onion's bulb is a potent fact and useful metaphor—the powerful, pearly layers upon layers, grown in the dark of the soil, swaddling a good cry. Diaphanous tissue of cells taut with rain, transmuted into aromatic, stinging juice, which, in a heated encounter with butter, yield the most alluring of the kitchen's perfumes.

I have been a gourmet cook, but not anymore. These days, I don't follow recipes. Usually the ingredients at hand determine the dish. The celery soup came to be because there had been an abundance of apples in the house the week before. I'd bought the celery to dice a few ribs into a Waldorf salad. Snacking my way through the rest of the celery didn't appeal. Utilizing it all in one fell soup seemed the more practical and pleasurable thing to do. Respecting food, preparing it nicely, set me thinking about hospitality, covenants, and friendships.

Although in this instance I was cooking for myself, there's nothing I like better than cooking for friends.

It's entirely apt that the title of one of the classic cookbooks speaks of the joy of cooking, all that sensuous, creative pleasure that precedes the joy of eating. Working hours are longer, life's pace has increased brutally, and children are booked solid with sports and other extracurricular activities. To be robbed of time for the enjoyable and ultimately convivial work that can be done in the kitchen and shared at the table certainly bespeaks a social ill, a destitution in affluence.

Learning to cook is a lifetime sport. In times of bounty, the culinary possibilities are inspirational and call for feasting. In lean times, parsimony with the parsnips, hunger as a seasoning, and remembering to say grace may all make the meal. Life's too short to forgo the gentle smiles that come of fondling eggplants and tomatoes, of being lost in a cloud of steam rising from a colander full of draining pasta, of drawing in the aroma of onions sautéing in butter. Of course, cooking is work. But it can be play at the same time and can reunite some of the scattered pieces of living. Like any endeavor, it's a lot more gratifying if it's undertaken freely and is not some thankless indenture. As with voluntary simplicity itself, volition makes all the difference.

My mother was a good and enthusiastic cook who just plain loved food. What I learned from her was not how to cook but that cooking can be an absorbing activity. Mama rarely accepted help in the kitchen, but she didn't mind a little company. She and her family had lived through the Great Depression in a small town in southern Mississippi. Her mother was a good cook, and her father was a doctor whose patients sometimes paid their bills in chickens or watermelons. There were other wonderful makings to be had: fish from the Gulf of Mexico, vegetables grown in household gardens and on nearby farms. Hunger was not a part of my mother's youth, even in the lean times. She ate at a big table where her mother fed ten or twelve at dinner: father, brother, sister-in-law, sisters, brothers-in-law, and their children.

My visits to Grandmother Garrison at her home in Mississippi were so long ago—she was so old and I was so young—that I can't recollect any of the meals. However, I keep in my wallet a scrap of ruled paper, one of my octogenarian aunt Madge's menus. Madge, Mama's older sister, cooked the following for a family dinner on the occasion of one of my visits to her home in Mobile, Alabama: butter beans, fresh fried corn, field peas, corn bread, dressing, roast, gravy, rice, Waldorf salad, and creamed potatoes for my second-cousin Josh, who got his special preferences. All of it was delicious, if not heart-smart. Perhaps it harked back to Grandmother's style of cooking.

Mama headed for New Orleans, the nearest big city, when she graduated from college. There, I imagine, she experienced a standard of cuisine that was pretty good even if the eatery happened to be the po'boy shop downstairs from the French Quarter apartment she shared with her sister Weesie, or the tea room at the Maison Blanche department store.

Mama read *Gourmet* magazine and clipped recipes from the *Phoenix Gazette*. When I was still a baby, she learned to make Mexican food from Mrs. Musa, our Mexican landlady. She swapped recipes with the *bonne vivant* Weesie and occasionally made dishes, such as coconut cake, fried chicken, or "Depression spaghetti," that her mother, Mattie, used to make. My mother the perfectionist boldly tried new things. She liked nothing better than the challenge of preparing some new dessert or canapé. With Dad, she would mount the occasional grand project, such as a huge batch of dark fruitcake for the holidays. This required toasting a washtub full of flour, beating a sweet, caloric wealth of butter, eggs, and sugar, and then folding a king's ransom of jewel-like glacéed fruit into the batter.

Mom and Dad enjoyed entertaining. My mother adopted an Emily Post etiquette and a style of table-setting established at a time when middle-class households had servants. Having no servants, Mama had to perform as cook, butler, and chatelaine for her dinner parties, with good help from her husband and help that was either grudging or substandard from her daughter.

My parents' entertaining was business-related. My father worked as a sales engineer for a foundry that made specialized castings for the hard-rock mining industry. Dad, whose father was a mining engineer and mine manager, had grown up in mining towns and gone to school with many of his customers. For all its geographic span, western mining seemed to be a small world. The conviviality in these circles was the genuine article. The 1950s, when Dad was establishing his career, were the days when rather than being VPs, MDs, JDs, or asset managers, wives were themselves assets. My vastly overqualified mother, with her honors baccalaureate degree and her administrative experience as a captain in the Women's Army Corps, poured herself into the homemaker role. Decades of great meals and memorable evenings were among her accomplishments. The hospitality at the Millses' was good.

After I graduated from college and had my first opportunity to cook on my own, I unconsciously let my mother's sensibility inform me and dove off the high board into *Mastering the Art of French Cooking* by Simone Beck, Louisette Bertholle, and Julia Child. Besides recipes for all manner of delicious dishes, the book provides good basic instruction in culinary technique. There are sensible explanations of the behavior of various foodstuffs at different temperatures and in different cooking media and some savory principles for combining herbs and spices with basic ingredients. Julia Child's jovial zest for cooking reinforced that diva-with-a-hearty-appetite approach to cuisine I'd observed back home.

Not long after I set up housekeeping, I was given an opportunity and a subsidy to do some fancy cooking and entertaining. Point Foundation, the eccentric nonprofit organization established to disperse the windfall profits from sales of the last *Whole Earth Catalog,* provided me with a grant to hold what it called a salon. Once or twice a week, I would organize a dinner party around a particular theme. We had a land reform seder, for example. Then I'd sit back as the guests, ecological activists mostly, who might be meeting one another for the first time, discussed and disputed their tangent interests and concerns over a meal of my preparing. Like my factotum mother, I was housemaid, butler, chef, sommelier, chatelaine, and scullion at these affairs.

I devoted myself to the salons and made some elaborate dishes, serving meals that included everything from soup to nuts, whose several courses I cooked single-handedly in the kitchen of my Berkeley, California, flat. The guests were seated at a table made from a door, on a motley assortment of used chairs unified by a coat of red paint. Napery was paisley—an Indian bedspread for the tablecloth, bandanas for napkins. There were always candles and flowers. We would sit and chat and eat for hours.

Like poetry, good dinner parties are conscious of form, if only to be able artfully to dispense with certain aspects of it. One formula for successful dinner parties holds that the guests should number no fewer than the Graces (three) and no more than the Muses (nine). Whether the audience is only me and a friend or two or a full eight at the table with all the dining chairs, leaves, and hodgepodge of crockery and linen pressed into service, cooking is a performing art, entertaining to the cook, certainly. Whatever the form, a dinner should be spacious and comfortable; the courtesy liberating, not intimidating. Entertaining should unobtrusively set the scene for pleasant surprises among the guests: insights, eloquence, wit, and the possibility of greater friendship.

Although those salon repasts were ample and the menus sometimes exotic, neither of those qualities is required for good hospitality. Epicurus in his garden, offering guests fresh water and barley porridge, demonstrated that the practice of hospitality is a simple matter. One can be penniless and still generous. Penniless or no, both guest and host can be embarrassed by intemperate hospitality.

Both my parents were, and Dad still is, hospitable by nature, courteous, and considerate of company. They taught hospitality by good example, by performing the countless small deeds—such as greeting guests at the door and immediately making them comfortable and offering refreshment— that declare and sustain the welcome. Hospitality means being mindful of the whole situation: having the home tidy, being attractively turned out, knowing or quickly learning something of the guests, making everyone feel included and looked after, and making an enjoyable time of it. Hospitality should be like manna from heaven, like grace, should feel as easy as breath.

Long after the salon stipend was discontinued, I cooked and hosted in my various San Francisco digs. The San Francisco Bay Area, with its geographic endowments of sea, estuary, and hinterlands even now productive of an extraordinarily diverse agricultural bounty, and with its mélange of cultures, is a foodie's promised land. During most of my years in the city, I lived within walking distance of Chinatown. It was a weekend treat to go there to do some marketing. Although I enjoyed Chinese cuisine, I never attempted it myself. The town was full of Chinese chefs doing a great job at scores of reasonably priced restaurants, and at that time I was cooking Creole and Mediterranean along with Southern home-style food. The essential genius of Chinese cuisine, though, with its rigorous insistence on freshness, authenticity, and seasonal appropriateness of ingredients and the deft relation to the flame, can inform any kind of cooking.

The Chinatown stores and shops that provision the Chinese community's home cooking provided me with a weekly sense banquet. I'd walk down Stockton Street, the main artery of the market, on Saturdays—market day. Sidewalks narrowed by buckets of live fish and tubs of freshwater clams, faced with poulterers dangling dead ducks and displaying pounds of chicken feet for sale, crowded with grocers arraying bok choy, foot-long string beans, and eel-like eggplants on tiers of crates, were another world to me. The sights and shouts and abattoir shocks feasted me as I was carried along the sidewalk by the throng of Chinese shoppers. They recognized everything, I assumed, and knew how to use the dried roots, tubers, and fish and the welter of noodles and potherbs and thousand-year eggs. Although I was just a kind of tourist, ignorant of the language and so comprehending only a fraction of what I beheld, I was marketing and I loved it.

Maybe the reason America has been so gulled by free-market rhetoric is that there's some recollection of real markets like the one in Chinatown, where consumers meet producers or vendors face to face and side by side and can compare goods differing in price, quality, and provenance in order to strike the best deal. At an appropriate scale, "the market" works. And the hands that supply and buy are out in the open. It's a communal encounter.

By the time I moved to the upper Midwest, I had eaten and cooked a sufficiency of blockbuster gourmet meals. A

good thing it was, too. I'd come to live in a Hovel in the heartland with two manly vegetarians, whole foods co-op activists.
The home cooking was hearty and delicious, anything but
recherché. Refinement was hooted out the door. I was, however, no stranger to spuds and tofu. In the early 1970s, I had
lived just a few blocks from the now-defunct Berkeley Co-op.
I was a member and did most of my shopping there. Interest
in healthy eating was part of the counterculture, and I had my
innings with Adelle Davis and her *Let's Cook It Right*.
Nonetheless, I had a lot to learn about whole foods cooking,
and Phil, who was a good cook, and Rob, an actual caterer,
taught me the ways of tempeh, nutritional yeast, and available
materials cuisine. The Hovel garden produced rhubarb,
spinach, zucchini, tomatoes, and basil well. We improvised,
cooking whatever vegetable jumped into our hands, eating our
way through the crop and moving on to the next ripe thing.

The bulk of our diet, and I use the term *bulk* advisedly, was
purchased in pounds at our natural foods cooperative. The co-
op, now more than twenty years old and flourishing, was
organized by some pioneering counterculturalists who needed
a reasonably priced supply of rolled oats, wheat germ, brown
rice, and the like and were willing to do the work to establish
an alternative emporium in their community. It started as a
buying club in a second-floor walk-up in Boardman City and
has grown to occupy 5,300 feet of floor space in a building
rehabilitated by an energy-conscious contractor who was willing to utilize unskilled but able members' labor to accomplish
the process.

Similar motives of economic self-reliance have been the
impetus for the establishment of consumer cooperatives since
the mid-nineteenth century. The form was invented back then
by twenty-nine English weavers in peaceful and constructive
rebellion at their having been gouged to pay for shoddy goods

and adulterated staples at the company store. These Rochdale pioneers pooled their savings and joined forces to purchase and sell various necessities at affordable prices, founding the first permanent consumer cooperative in 1844.

Co-ops represent a middle way in economic enterprise, practicing group ownership, group governance, group responsibility, and a commitment to democratic principles and member education. Thus, our local natural foods co-op, in addition to keeping us in kelp, spelt, and soy, is part of an ongoing social experiment in a long-standing tradition. The basic cooperative principles are that membership is open to all without discrimination, each member has one vote, the cooperative's earnings are distributed according to use, the return on member capital is limited, the cooperative offers its members some form of continuing education, cooperatives cooperate among themselves, and cooperatives work for the sustainable development of their communities.

To be actively involved in a cooperative is to dissent from the profit motive as business's paramount drive and from the structural irresponsibility of corporations. Implicit dissent and democratic practice attract the vociferous. One of my old friends from Berkeley, who'd been active in the Berkeley Co-op and had observed some of its rabid contretemps, developed a co-op theory of personality, to wit, cooperatives, especially food cooperatives, naturally attract oral types.

In addition to the initial purchase of a membership and the expenditure of breath in meetings and discussion, it is also possible to invest time in a cooperative. A few hours of cheese wrapping, shelf stocking, or newsletter editing earns a working member's discount and reduces one's food prices even further. Being a shareholder in our co-op is a participatory thing, and my participation has me rooting for the co-op's success. This is much different from the attitude of wary skepticism that colors my dealings with the big-box supermarket in the mall belt south of Boardman City.

Our enduring, occasionally contentious natural foods co-op has become a lively community institution—a marketplace where Seventh-day Adventists, survivalists, heart patients, vegans, aging hippies, and buffed yuppies mingle amid cornucopias of organic produce, bulk food bins, and a selection of shade-grown coffees and free-range eggs. Shopping at the co-op is, whether I'm in the mood or not, a social event. It's rare not to encounter one or two friends or acquaintances of long standing while shopping there.

Sometimes I take the co-op bonhomie a little too far and assume a degree of comradeship with all my fellow shoppers, even strangers. After all, whether they are members or not, they are straying off the supermarket track, with its glossily wrapped convenience, in pursuit of real food. They are dubious about at least one aspect of the dominant paradigm and want food that is grown without chemotherapy and sold with a minimum of processing and packaging. I gladly imagine that they're my kind of people. My approaching these neophyte shoppers as fellow conspirators may unnerve some of them, but it's an old co-op habit, 1970s nostalgia.

Belonging to the co-op is one of the commitments that has bound the local counterculture together over the years. I'm a latecomer to this counterculture, and so I admire my friends who twenty or more years ago were putting up their windmills, gardening organically, working for peace and against nuclear power, becoming midwives, and schooling their kids at home, in the days and in a place where being different was not, as it was for us in the Bay Area, expected or widely countenanced.

In the fall of 1986, when Phil and I were in the hospital struggling to survive our respective car-crash traumas, the co-op, where Rob and other close friends worked and which was visited frequently by most of the members of our larger circle, became the nerve center of our support system. The staff posted daily bulletins on Phil's condition, which was, for an agonizing week, critical. On any given day, one or two co-op members would check on me, and a lot of them were praying to a lively assortment of divinities for our healing. Our experience was not singular. There was always community building going on in the store, alongside the tofu and granola selling. Although co-ops are started for practical reasons, mutual aid is the fundamental covenant, and like neighborliness, it is a practice that can change lives in profound and definite ways.

Before I'd ever actually been part of any, I heartily propagandized the joys of community and the wisdom of small groups. I believed that these ways of working together offered us salvation. I still do, but I now know that the path to salvation inevitably leads through purgatory.

Egalitarian, democratic processes can be slow, confused, and confusing at best. So be it. Learning to work in groups through thick and thin is a necessity of citizenship and is the very sinew of activism. For years, I served on the co-op's board of directors. It was group process graduate school. A stint as board president was some of the hardest work I'd ever done. Two years featuring several committee meetings a week, plenty of phone calls, anxiety-racked nights, and the agonies of responsibility entailed in the effort to make the world safe for bulk granola led me to vow never again to oversimplify the reality of community or to romanticize group work.

Prior to this presidency, I had done some group facilitation. I had even studied consensus facilitation with Caroline Estes, a master of this nonhierarchal, nonmajoritarian group decision-making practice. That was the experience and skill I brought to the task of the collective governance of a natural foods grocery. No financial expertise, business sense, or political acumen sullied my thinking. Fortunately, the other members of the board had lashings of these. We worked pretty well together, attempting not so much to mind the store, which was the manager's job, as to fulfill our duty of responsible oversight. Most of our meetings were routine and comradely. We adopted consensus as our decision-making mode, which made meetings a little less parliamentary and a little more touchy-feely.

It fell to us, however, to resolve a long-standing management problem. The manager, a fine and much-liked person, had reached the limits of her capability in that position, and stagnation was becoming regression. After months of trying procedural remedies, imposing deadlines for new business plans, and spending thousands of dollars on consultants to procure the skills we thought we needed in order to avoid taking the miserably difficult step of dismissal, the board as a body snapped. After a particularly confounding executive committee meeting whose purpose was to try yet again to work things out, which purpose was yet again frustrated, we terminated the manager's employment in what was by then an uncharacteristically abrupt manner. Our action seriously riled the active portion of the co-op's membership (an energetic minority of people who were willing to participate in the co-op's affairs) and many staff members, who were naturally enough dismayed by the change and the loss of their colleague. From then on, all the board could do was show up and take the heat.

This meant sitting through unusually well attended meetings at which people we'd respected and worked with for years vented their outrage upon us. Old friends expressed their displeasure with our decision in heartfelt, eloquent ways. The amazing thing was that almost none of this passionate confrontation was acrimonious or ad hominem. Although there were personal loyalties as well as the greater good involved, something about the character of the group and the wisdom of the institution, the reality that we all shared the purpose of fostering the co-op, helped temper our conflict.

That face-to-face stuff is as real as community gets. Looking the person with whom you disagree right in the eye as you air your differences, looking on as somebody you've misunderstood or underestimated performs a feat of diplomacy or communication that retrieves a disintegrating meeting, being forgiven for being flat wrong about something, leaving the meeting chamber together and asking the person who moments ago disputed your judgment, "How's it going?"—and listening well because the answer to that question genuinely matters to you—all strengthen essential heart muscles as little else can. For this solitaire, "group" is the most demanding kind of work. I have to be part of something larger, not a soloist. In group work, my aspirations and abilities are enhanced, qualified, pruned, tempered, synergized, tactfully ignored, or welcomed by turns, as are everyone else's.

In my more cynical moments, I can fall prey to the impulse to ridicule the disproportionate sums of human energy and attention that our small-town natural foods cooperative consumes. Those moments pass, and I remind myself that to trivialize the small good things that we accomplish in community implies assent to the pernicious idea that bigger must be better.

What could be more basic and more urgent than a grassroots effort to relocalize our economies and food systems and to provide markets for organic farmers? Chain-store provender becomes more frightening by the minute, with its pesticide residues and waxes, weird additives such as nonfattening fats and synthetic flavors and colors, with its preference for cosmetic perfection over nutritional value, with its use of genetically modified plant and animal ingredients, with the antibiotics, bacteria, and possible mad cow prions in the beef, and with the irradiation of food to preserve it and the quantities of colorful plastic and cardboard that contain it. Nowadays when I bring some food item home from a supermarket, I think more in terms of sterilizing and decontaminating it than of cooking it.

In addition to concerns about our food's quality and value as nourishment, the tenuousness of the far-flung—indeed, globalized—food production and distribution system deserves some fretting over. This system's vulnerability to disruptions in transport and the vagaries of corporate proprietorship make the co-op's sometimes laborious efforts to buy locally, inform consumers, support an independent cooperative network of food production and distribution, and promote good nutrition seem not ludicrous at all.

Dismantling the mystique of bigness and questioning the notion that cheap food is a good buy, urging consumers to buy locally and support small farmers, empowering everyday people to participate in the provision of trustworthy food, and going about this work through democratic egalitarian group processes could make the difference between ours being a more resilient, self-reliant community and its being one that might fall into nasty disarray when the remote, centralized sources of capital and methodology fail, seize up, or move on.

Believing this with all my heart and honoring the work of our co-op's board, staff, and membership, I eventually came to a point of diminishing returns in my co-op board service. I'd gone to one meeting too many. The work wasn't eliciting my better nature, and I wasn't doing well in my attempts to do good. I had to quit volunteering and "get off the committee," as my friend Mercedes puts it. Yet voting myself a sabbatical from this and all my other do-gooder groups drastically reduced my occasions for spending time with my cohorts, role models, and cronies.

It has been a while since I've had a lover or a partner, and this is by and large a comfortable celibacy. Altogether, I've spent more of my adult years living by myself than in liaisons. Thus, friendships are the human relationships shaping and satisfying me now.

Many of my friends here and elsewhere are colleagues and comrades. We are friends through our sharing of a worldview and certain convictions. Living in this part of the country, away from the coastal capitals and big cities, I've become part of a small community, a counterculture that is intelligently activist about ecology, peace, diversity, and economic justice but is not an intelligentsia. My friends here are plenty smart, but most of them don't make their living as professional smart people, which was more the case back in the Bay Area in the 1970s, where *activist* was a job description and writers of my ilk were thick on the ground. Here, the activists tend to have day jobs.

If what brings us together might be termed politics, it's not the only thing we do among ourselves. We feed each other, throw parties, celebrate and commiserate, and show up with bouquets or casseroles, depending on the situation.

I stay linked with my California friends by telephone and the occasional jet. Friendships struck within the bioregional movement, at ecological restoration conferences, Luddite conclaves, and writers' workshops are carried on by fortuitous rendezvous or by correspondence. "Sir, more than kisses, letters mingle souls," wrote John Donne to Sir Henry Wotton, "for, thus friends absent speak." And so we do.

A person with friends need never be bored. There is always more to fathom and enjoy in the complexity of others, and always the possibility of finding a way to delight them. To listen as a friend articulates a problem, working it out as she or he talks, is both an honor and a prayerful act. All it takes is a closed mouth and an open heart. Of course, friendship takes time, merits time, beguiles the time. Not to be solitary in one's solitude but to know that the possibility of sharing a joke, some news, a swim, or an errand awaits outside the cloister gates, and to remember that the world that beckons is adorned with familiar faces, balances the contemplative life. Solitude is rich but seldom hilarious.

Thinking of this friend and that, near or far away, and of the ways our souls have mingled, makes me long to be with them, to hear that voice, to see that face, to embrace them, break bread together, and talk. "Most beautiful is the sight of those near and dear to us," said Epicurus, "when our original kinship makes us of one mind."

Within that kinship of like minds, still one can have a diverse array of friendships and friendships of many degrees. Despite understanding the pitfalls of idealism, I am an idealist, and I tend to idealize my friends. It makes for some rocky times when the reality of human limitations, thine and mine, impinges. That is the moment when love can arrive. Idealization mellows to simple respect. Acquaintance continues. Affection grows. Friendships offer good practice in accepting the transience of experience and the persistence of feeling.

Friendship entails no vows, contracts, or formal commitments. In fact, such strictures might work against the spirit of friendship, which is a freedom, and discerning: "We must not approve of either those who are always ready for friendship or those who hang back, but for friendship's sake we must even run risks," said Epicurus.

It may just be writerly to wring every trace of feeling and meaning from incident, but I experience a shadow side to friendship, a place where neglect, invidious comparison, envy, resentment, doubt, inadequacy, pining, and worry clatter around. I can't get enough of a friend until my attention shifts, and then I don't want to feel guilty about focusing elsewhere for a while. When I need to talk with somebody or want someone to come out and do something with me, and that person is unavailable, I'm momentarily aggrieved. I'm attracted to people whom I admire, and I find qualities to admire in those with whom I feel an affinity. Admiration, alas, can boomerang and catch me by the throat: I could never be as centered as C., as forthright as L., as grounded as S., as astute as A., as persistent as R., as strenuously honest as G., as bold as K., as severally talented as B., as sweet as J., a genius like P., as genuine as F., as hilarious as D., as steadfast as T.

Self-doubt is a plague. When I haven't heard from someone in a while—and for me, this is one of the moral hazards of epistolary friendships especially—I assume that I've blundered, given offense, and incurred a cold, silent wrath. I mentioned this habit of mind to my current shrink, and she said, "Maybe that's because anger is preferable to indifference." What chagrin to discover that I could resent my friends for apparently, even actually, not thinking of me. As with romances, I've had to learn that friendships are not improved by clinging or control.

If I am good, it's the result of co-evolving with my friends. "My mind is lovely as a spruce," wrote Michael McClure, "and I and those that love me make it mine." My friends have given such gifts to me—hard truths that I could somehow hear; succor; hilarity; stories; and company. Longtime friendships are supremely precious: To support friends in triumph and sorrow, to fool around with them, delight in their gifts, learn from their virtues and their offhand remarks, to witness time's passage in the life of someone known and close, is a revelation through the saga of the everyday—the gray hairs, the grandchildren, the parents and pets buried, the works accomplished and ailments endured, the deepening more evident in others than in oneself. Sharing the satisfactions of decades together may be the sweetest feeling of all.

"Of all the things which wisdom acquires to produce the blessedness of the complete life," said Epicurus, "far the greatest is the possession of friendship." A friendship incarnates the pleasure of a life well lived. Friendship is more than thee and more than me. It is that third thing—greater than the sum of the parts, incapable of existing without the parties to it. As the sage Helen Luke was wont to point out, Interest is *inter est*. It arises between self and others. You show up and show yourself to another; attend to, enjoy, respond to your friend; and expect a third for the feast.

Being an only child and without issue, I'm short on kin and need my friends, cleave to my old friends, and am happy to embark on new friendships. I try to be a good friend and always wish to be a better one. As this life of mine continues, the estate of friendship is beginning to loom like a holy mountain over the hills and dales of romance. Forgiveness seems to be at the heart of it—self-forgiveness, so that one's offer of oneself in friendship is nothing mean—and compassion and detachment enough to forgive the other for failing to attend one's ego's every want and need. There are always mistakes along the way. To awaken from my trance of self-absorption to the tenderness and invitation to love in some person whom I've feared or condescended to or thought beyond my ken happens rarely enough, but it's a big epiphany, and to matter and bring something good to the life of someone I cherish is consummation aplenty.

In the hard times that are coming, we will need to be good friends. Once I heard my friend Chellis, a woman of remarkable courage and vision, suggest that perhaps our mission now

is like that of the American Indians at the height of the geno-
cide in the late nineteenth century. At that point, there was no
question of winning the battle. What remained to be done was
to keep hold of what it meant to be human.

7

VOCATION

One evening over dinner, Michelle, a friend who teaches in the early grades, mentioned that a pupil of hers, a little girl, had that very day become literate and realized it. "I can read!" she shouted. "I can read!" Michelle had done the teaching, but only the child herself could have done the learning. Her life changed utterly in that moment when the characters on the page made sound, then words, and then meaning in her mind.

One door opens, another closes. Literacy admits us to civilization and to the pleasures of reading and writing, to the treasures of literature and the intrigue of research. It also forecloses the possibility of experiencing the other, less abstract ways of learning and knowing, of the personal communication and cultural chronicling of oral cultures. Literacy shapes a consciousness that renders the world into words, requires a focus on the page.

I can barely remember not reading. Before I could read, I was being read to, insisting on it. Mom and Dad obliged me, returning to each week's Little Golden Book again and again. I can't remember my reading epiphany. Whenever it was, reading became the leading passion of my life.

Reading makes it possible to visit, even inhabit, the cosmopolis of literate minds and meet the likes of Rebecca West. At one point in *Black Lamb and Grey Falcon,* her discursive virtuoso travelogue of her journeys in the Balkans between the First and Second World Wars, West remarks that "any writer worth his salt knows that only a small proportion of literature does more than partly compensate people for the damage they have suffered by learning to read." Brilliant a writer as she was, West knew literacy was a sword that cuts both ways. So saying, she put herself and any writer who reads her on notice that to create a work that actually realizes literature's best possibility is a feat exceedingly rare.

It is, I suspect, the feat that every writer worth her salt desires to achieve. Those desires batten on written works that in the writer's hermetic milieu of incessant reading, writing, and internal narration utterly remake the world.

West's observation hints at the world remaking—or unmaking—that literate societies wish upon oral cultures and on the natural world, their ground of being. The written word is the most decisive of all human technologies, allowing our communication to transcend place and time intact—writ in stone or clay, given mass circulation by hot type and printer's ink. Disembodied ideas, military orders, propaganda, legal codes, dogma, shibboleth, and the objectification of the living world can all, once written, be projected at imperial scale.

At a time when information-besotted human beings are both deliberately and inadvertently causing the death of countless other species—and "for one species to mourn the death of another," as Aldo Leopold said, "is a new thing under the sun"—I find an awful lot to regret in human history, especially its latest chapters. Except for those plants and animals we've thoroughly domesticated, none of the other life-forms really needs us. What redeems our tenure on the planet?

Along with loving-kindness, I nominate art. Literature is my favorite art form, although I wouldn't want to be deprived of any of the others. Reading *Lord Jim* was as exotic and life-shaping a sojourn for me as a trip to India, and I have made one of those. In museums there, I wandered among realms of artistic treasures, from exquisite tribal fish traps to supple Natarajas, images of the dancing Shiva evoked in stone. In Benares, I sat on a temple rooftop listening to a high priest's music lesson. He was learning to sing the names of God. In all this vast swirl of inspired human expression, however unfamiliar the idiom, the historic moment, or the dramatic circumstance, artistic truth galvanizes the soul.

Be it sculpture, poetry, or narrative fraught with terrible insight, hymns or temples to divinity, harvest songs or hand-made tools anonymously perfected in tradition and function, art does endure. It troubles and pleases, inspires, and reminds us that humanity is ever capable of adding to the sum of the world's grave beauty.

If truth is beauty, then George Orwell's work may also be called beautiful. Orwell's "Why I Write" is one of the surest, truest explanations of accepting the fate of being a writer I've yet read. The "four great motives for writing . . . prose," he says, are "sheer egoism, esthetic enthusiasm, historical impulse, and political purpose."

Orwell recalls the primary literary activity of his school years, "the making up of a continuous 'story' about myself, a sort of diary existing only in the mind," which had a "meticulous, descriptive quality," and he notes the early onset of the writerly habits of self-observation and self-absorption, of self-importance and the strange conviction that what occurs to one, within and without, deserves to be told, and told well.

Nobody asked me to be a writer, but I wrote for publication as soon as I was able. In the first grade, I got my hand slapped with a ruler for circulating a one-page satirical newspaper in the back rows of the classroom.

I write because I can. I write because I am interested in my inchoate thoughts and in the elucidation of thought that writing can achieve. I write because I am word-drunk. I write because by now, that's mainly what I do. There may not be a story about myself, with a meticulous, descriptive quality, being made up in my mind, but there is a carnival of language and opinion, judgment, speculation, wisecracks, and incessant curiosity.

Curiosity is my daemon. The insatiable, promiscuous magpie mind wants to know. Of all the reference works that surround me, the dictionary is my best beloved. In "Why I Write," Orwell speaks of taking "pleasure in the impact of one sound on another." Finding the rightest word for a given purpose, however underutilized that word may be, is some of the best fun I have in writing. Not everyone enjoys a trip to the dictionary, though, and some readers and editors have complained of my sesquipedalian style. It is said that the American vocabulary has declined by half in the past few decades. It's a tragic instance of desertification following upon monocultural commodity production, the clear-cutting of written and spoken English. To write with as much of this agile, affluent language as I know or can learn, then, could be construed as a kind of conservation activity, like saving and planting heirloom seeds.

Writing what I want to write about—things that matter to me—and pursuing my curiosity, or "home-schooling my inner child," as my friend Amy Elena put it, is a kind of luxury. It is also a choice I cannot help but make. Yet I wonder: Does everyone feel as anxious to justify their lives as I do? Do all writers? I am leading a life endowed, and not by the sweat of my brow alone, with a relative abundance of time and freedom. I find the time to reflect, to write letters to friends, to read good books, to cook and serve the occasional meal, to go for a walk, to pet the cat. I make time to write down my dreams, to tidy up the house.

I have time to write in my journal while single mothers scrape by, desperate for a moment's privacy; time to peruse the classics while the college student holds down a couple of jobs to pay off student loans; time to make a dish from scratch while some working folks at this end of the county must supplement their diet with the canned goods the postmistress collects. There can be no justification for such disparities, let alone the disparity between a life like mine and that of a Bill Gates.

Writing is a vocation as ecology is a vocation. In earlier times, people with a religious vocation were understood to be so married to their calling that to have an earthly spouse would be unfair. What's more, there was the martyrdom factor to consider. To take a whole family along to the stake or into the coliseum would have thinned out the ranks of the faithful. As my former beau Harry, the Zen beekeeper, put it, "We make the sacrifices we can"; we try to make the best choice from among starkly contending alternatives. One has to be something of a hermit to write. The choice I made when I was twenty-one not to have children bought me a lot of time and freedom. Yet the writing, dissenting life is famously insecure. Around deadline time, it's notoriously unrewarding for the writer's intimate associates. Although I've met quite a few people who think they want to be writers, I doubt that "writer's spouse" is high on anybody's list of life choices.

Much of the endeavor of writing is in developing and sustaining a kind of trance. It requires large blocks of uninterrupted hours. It becomes necessary to turn off the telephone and decline invitations, which causes me to miss my friends and hope that they'll still be there when I resurface. The struggle against a hydra of distraction, temptation, and interruption feels Herculean. I become miserly about my time and feel it hemorrhaging in every phone conversation and chat with a friend encountered in the course of an errand.

Once solitude is achieved, the demarcation between writing and not writing becomes a broken line. While I'm washing dishes, stitching a patchwork, sweeping the house, making cookies, or riding my bike, I am solving those problems that resist a frontal approach. Thinking wants leisure. That may be why workaholism, the commodity spectacle, and minimum-wage employment together constrict the social, civic, and aesthetic imagination. Every person possesses worthy intelligence and creativity; circumstance can debase or entirely silence it. Time clocks rob the world of wild possibility. That's what they're for.

It's the artist's duty to have an artist's life, somehow to obtain time and freedom and then to muster the desire and discipline to make good work out of the life, whether that goodness is in the work's aesthetics, its radicalism, its candor, its singularity, or its universality.

Not writing puts me off my feed. I've kept a journal for twenty years in order to have a diary and a confidante and to be writing, regardless. "Nothing gets me going like the deadline or the check" is a saying attributed to Duke Ellington, and it applies to me. I'd continue to write without an assignment, but I doubt I'd ever rewrite or finish anything. Every piece of writing I've ever completed, even for high school and college newspapers and literary magazines, has been on a deadline.

That discipline to get the thing done and cut it loose, finally, has required sustained and contractual encouragement from external forces.

Writing is a desk job, hard on the body in the sedentary way. Eyestrain, writer's cramp, and an above-average anxiety level are among the hazards of the trade. If you want to know how difficult writing can *seem* to be, consider the fact that a not particularly flexible woman in her early fifties would rather spend a few hours incurring the aches and pains that come from splitting and stacking firewood or shoveling snow than sit indoors on a cushioned chair with a cup of tea at hand and confront a manuscript in need of revision.

The world is so rich in distractions, and I am so poor in concentration. I shuttle back and forth constantly between my studio and my house—to fetch or excrete another cup of tea or just to turn away from the page for a moment and move about. Once I'm parked at the desk, ready to begin, I haul out the typewriter or the ruled letter pad and go. I try to get "it" all down. Generating five or six pages is a solid evening's work; enough such evenings and a first draft appears. Anne Lamott, in her writing wisdom, says that first drafts are always terrible. Or they may be good first drafts but should not be let stand.

As the deadline approaches, the book or essay begins to develop its own life. Passages start waking me up. The pad and pencil are waiting by the bed: it's better not to make the muse wait upon such pettiness as washing up, getting dressed, and making breakfast. Then it's time for revision, for taking pencil to paper and inserting, deleting, finding a better word or sequence of phrases. I keep before me Isaac Bashevis Singer's observation that "the wastepaper basket is the writer's best friend." I cut out paragraphs and sentences, move them around, paste them down, or ditch them. At first, this work appals me. Many games of solitaire may be required before I can make myself begin the insurmountable task and put the first mark on the typescript.

The reader may be wondering whether updated equipment might not expedite the process. Working people, of course, need the appropriate tools of their trade. I just wish to continue working with the tools with which I began. When I write, I sit in my little freestanding room, writing in pencil on a letter pad. The artificial sunlight of a seasonal affective disorder (SAD) lamp blazes in my face and on the page, possibly fooling my pineal gland as to what season it actually is.

Having rounded life's midpoint, I feel like Rip van Winkle in need of another sleeping pill. Years ago, when I left San Francisco, I came to this place hoping that the mere fact of residing in the country would confer upon me the virtues of Helen and Scott Nearing and cause me to live the good life. My life is good, although not, by Nearing standards, simple. Still, I've been able to isolate myself from certain technological changes. I escaped the world of office work just at the moment when computer literacy became mandatory and *workstation* synonymous with *computer screen*. Because I work for myself and am one of the rare employers who doesn't require computer proficiency, I've been able to avoid purchasing and learning to use a personal computer.

Currently, to earn the Luddite epithet one doesn't have to break machines, just forgo them. I've withstood years of being nagged to write with a personal computer. My reply is that the difficulty of writing is not technical. There's no way to make it easy. A portable manual typewriter, mechanical pencils, scissors, tape, telephone, legal pads, the services of a typist, various libraries, and the mailbox all work well for me. So far, these vintage means have allowed me to write a few books and scores of lectures, essays, and book reviews and to take care of business and communicate with friends and family. If it ain't broke, why fix it?

I typed the manuscript of my first book myself. An extremely psychoanalytic process it was, requiring three weeks of careful pecking on a rented electric typewriter. The worst part was the exhausting argument with a pandemonium of self-doubt clothing itself in the form of the meanest, most sardonic, supercilious, and impossible-to-please book critics in the land, all reading over my shoulder. The gist of my rejoinders was, "Yeah, this may be the most jejune, self-serving, euphuistic, hippy-dippy book a reviewer's ever seen, but at least it will have reached the publisher near the deadline. Thank you for sharing."

That was the last paper manuscript unaccompanied by a floppy disk I was allowed to submit. For the next three books, I worked with Sue, a wonderful typist and word-processing adept. It wasn't practical economics but a saving grace to have Sue, with her shrewd wit, good humor, and top-of-the-line personal computer as party to the isolated, bordering on autistic, process of writing a book.

This manuscript will have been typed and digitized by Marcy, a book-loving Luddite whose day job is medical transcription. When she is not plying her skills at the keyboard, Marcy is building a log cabin from the stone foundation up, mostly by hand. She lived for a while at the site of her cabin without benefit of electricity and running water and commuted to the office where her word-processing equipment was housed. Lately, she and her partner, Patrick, are living in a more conventional dwelling while they complete the cabin. There they raise Jacob sheep and grow their own vegetables. In addition to the transcription and typing she does for me, Marcy cans, spins, and knits. It's a gift to know someone like Marcy, who does such a good job of walking her talk.

I would far rather my money go to the likes of Marcy and Sue (who give me the starving artist discount) than to a computer manufacturer or software publisher.

The computer industry, like much other consumer-product manufacture, depends on poorly paid and poorly protected third-world labor, much of it female, to keep the wares afford-able. What's more, it generates a lot of toxic waste, about forty-nine pounds per typical computer, according to John C. Ryan and Alan Thein Durning's invaluable *Stuff: The Secret Lives of Everyday Things.*

None of my contemporaries is likely to be able to craft a personal computer from scratch in the basement (nor a pencil, as my friend Tom pointed out, although Thoreau could do the latter). Nobody is ever going to have a personal computer that doesn't profit a corporation. That this is characteristic of a lot of mass technologies, including good ol' telephones, is not an argument in favor of computers. After years of defending what may seem to be an illogical or inconsistent refusal to employ this technology on my premises but not on somebody else's, all I can say is "Tell it to the Amish." If religious sects can, for their own reasons, make discriminating choices about the technologies they'll adopt—the last time I followed an Amish buggy, it had rubber tires—why can't individuals?

These days, folks are chewing on me about not having e-mail capability. I have no ambition to "converse" casually with thousands of total strangers or, through e-mail, to increase the volume of correspondence I leave unattended. Communication deserves care. I want to be able to see the faces of those with whom I converse, to offer them hospital-ity if we're at my place or to bring a little gift to theirs. The telephone is a pale substitute, but the voice still carries a vol-ume of nonverbal communication, and it allows for give-and-take in real time.

In correspondence, I want to put pen to paper and write to a person. The action of writing is a link to the earliest scribes. Handwriting itself can be a form of artistic self-expression. It's certainly a means of self-disclosure. Handwriting analysis wouldn't be so uncannily accurate if that were not so. There is even a small art in the choice of postage stamps. Postal correspondence is full of suspense. It has me racing out to the mailbox six days a week, hoping to find a personal letter.

How unsettling it was a decade or more ago to receive, for the first time, a personal letter justified and typeset in some kind of book font—not even a ragged right-hand margin. It looked like a public document, but it was some priceless correspondence from Jay Kinney, a superb essayist, publisher, and underground cartoonist. It was signed in his good hand, and the typography didn't diminish his provocative thought. In my response, I mentioned my consternation. Jay's next letter came set in a cursive font. Since then, many good and treasured personal letters have come neatly justified and printed out. Being aware that printing out, addressing, and posting have begun to feel onerously labor-intensive to e-mailers, I am abjectly grateful to have them.

Many people I respect and admire, young activists and organizers especially, are making brilliant use of their laptop computers and the Internet, and I can't fault them. Forgoing a computer remains my preference, though. I don't renounce this technology lightly or without understanding the risk of impending isolation. Many good friends and colleagues are navigating well in cyberspace while I'm hunched at my desk like a diehard Latin speaker or manuscript scribe paring her goose quills while the printing presses are starting to issue works in vernacular language.

By making this choice, to forgo quantity and expanse of information and communication in order to retain familiar qualities and limitations in my life, I wind up being a squatter under the off-ramp of the information superhighway, watching many of my friends and colleagues speed by. Is it mulish of me not to drive the fastest vehicle I can, even if I have to get a real job to make the payments?

"I spit upon luxurious pleasures, not for their own sake, but because of the inconveniences that follow them," said Epicurus. The most computer-savvy people I know are always pining for more megabytes and better software. "Enough" seems to be unavailable in the new economy. It may be an information age, but planned obsolescence is a chump's game. It takes more work to earn more money to be overwhelmed by more information that does not equal knowledge or wisdom. Thanks to computers, it's become necessary to do that work with ever-increasing speed, purported efficiency, and digitally demanded uniformity.

"Real yogis do their own work," says my friend Roger, who's an organic farmer, Iyengar yoga instructor, and all-around athlete. Wendell Berry does his own work horse-farming in Kentucky. Helen and Scott Nearing went about *Living the Good Life* by doing a quotient of "bread labor"—gardening, house building, maple sugaring—neatly calculated to allow them also to engage in "head labor." To underwrite the writing, the bread labor has to produce the necessities.

Back in 1984, my theory was that I would just paint myself into a corner of virtue and adapt. Living a more austere and earth-friendly life would follow upon rustication. Hubby would help me learn, by my fortieth birthday, to hang loose, self-rely, do more with less. Instead, a broad vein of princess in my character, running counter to the rough-and-ready homesteader ambition, came to light. From the beginning, there was a lot of hard work, such as pulling nails from salvaged lumber, sanding, painting, and other studio-building activities, that I didn't much care to learn how to do.

Early on, then, I followed the principle of comparative advantage and returned to my wordly pursuits. I slipped swiftly back to my specialty of writing. I could bend my energies to the familiar, ply my writing skills for the usual meager earnings, or I could do amateurishly a whole bunch of little jobs around the Hovel or the new homesite, contributing, at going rates, unskilled labor worth perhaps the price of a tank of gas every week.

I stayed choosy about which parts of my own work I would do. I would do some snow shoveling, some wood splitting and stacking, some gardening sporadically. This begs the question: What if we do our own work as a kind of literary or ethical conceit? What if we do some of our own heavy lifting and it cannot possibly be sufficient to meet our bohemian needs, let alone wants, even after these have been trimmed? I've tried something as simple as growing some of my own food, and at the end of a full day's work at it was so stove up and exhausted that sitting in a dazed stupor was the only capability left. I don't know how Scott and Helen did it. No doubt they were early risers.

The connection between my vocation and my livelihood has never been direct. The kind of writing I want and love to do pays poorly when it pays at all. The cause-oriented publishers and periodicals whose output may be short on sensation and celebrity, but not on consequence or quality, that do me the honor of publishing my work tend to remunerate their authors in the low three and four figures or with warm gratitude. Their operations depend on canny editors who know how to invite an essay, book review, or full-blown book in such a thought-provoking way that pecuniary considerations seem beside the point.

With time spent writing and speaking, I earn some federal dollars. The balance of my livelihood comes as a gift from the philanthropy of individuals and institutions. There have been gifts and grants, and the mangled leg endowment, to make up the difference between what I am paid for my writing and what I think I need to live on. When people ask me how I support myself by writing, I can't honestly say that I do.

Public speaking has been a part of my livelihood for the past thirty years. Although I have done it hundreds of times, I still get terribly strung out before giving a talk. There are usually a few nights of insomnia occupied with the puzzle of recombining various pieces of my wardrobe in ways that will be interesting to me, at least. I enjoy dressing up, figuring out a costume that won't highlight the sweat stains spreading out from my armpits. This prodrome means that I'm usually sleep-deprived, adrenalized, and hyper long before I park my car at the Boardman City airport and submit to the dismal expedient of jet travel.

Because I talk about a variety of subjects—sense of place, voluntary simplicity, ecological restoration, and nature writing—to assorted audiences, from community groups to learned conferences, I don't have a stock talk. Every time I stand at a lectern, my remarks are new to me. Whenever you give a speech, they say, it's actually three speeches: the speech you intend to give, the speech you do give, and the speech you wish you had given. All three of them seem to entail inordinate amounts of energy, but it's the work on the last one that usually does me in.

Lots of people apparently believe that a world without intellectuals and artists would be not only tolerable but preferable. Pol Pot and Chairman Mao come to mind, and, through their sins of omitting to tax and fund, the United States Congress and most state legislatures. The mass market would seem to argue that there's not enough effective demand for writing that seeks to do more than divert. Much-bally-

hooed multimillion-dollar advances notwithstanding, nobody
I know in this business is getting rich. Yet there are enough
ardent, intelligent readers whose need for such writing is
real—and, miraculously, enough editors and publishers
upholding an intellectual commitment to issue challenging
works—that the good books keep appearing. It is possible to
consumerize the pleasures of books and reading, but as long
as there are libraries, the cosmopolis of literacy, far-flung in
space and time, remains a commons.

If one's heart lives where one's treasures are laid up, then
my heart's shelved somewhere between *A Natural History of
Trees* and *A Sand County Almanac.* I've been acquiring books
for thirty years, not least as a hedge against a dystopic, book-
burning future of the sort Ray Bradbury envisioned in *Fahrenheit 451.* In my apocalyptic fantasy, I envision my disparate
library as the foundation of Ms. Mills' Eclectic Academy,
where the chandeliers of civilization could be kept twinkling
through the coming dark age. My household is crowded with
books, not all of them good nor all of them read. In my writing studio, the shelving crisis is acute. Apart from a *Collected
Works of William Shakespeare,* the studio library consists of
works of nonfiction, the tools of my trade. There, I'm immured
by field guides, reference books, dictionaries, anthologies, collections of interviews with ecological thinkers, nature writing,
environmental history, alternative economics, natural history,
voluntary simplicity, devolutionary politics, neo-Luddism,
anthropology, human ecology, social criticism, maps, back
issues of *CoEvolution Quarterly,* and six file cabinets' worth of
correspondence and materials gathered for past, present, and
ongoing projects.

In the house, there are collections of essays, a shelf of
books on psychology with a Jungian cast, and a shelf of philosophy and religion. There is a shelf of cookbooks, and there

are a couple of shelves of biography and memoir and a couple of shelves of underutilized poetry. I've been hauling around my priceless collection of *Mad* paperbacks since I left home and have accumulated books of cartoons by Lynda Barry, Nina Paley, and George Booth. I've got volumes of *Krazy Kat, Pogo,* and *Uncle Scrooge.* There are a bracing couple of shelves of feminist works and the complete Starhawk; I have a little collection on salons, one on India, another on Tarot. Books inscribed to me by their authors help furnish my home, as do near-complete sets of the detective novels of Dorothy Sayers and Ross MacDonald. There are growing numbers of works by Joseph Conrad, Charles Dickens, George Orwell, and Rebecca West. There are scores of novels awaiting a first or second encounter.

When people tell me I should check out the Internet and see what I'm missing, I say loftily, "Not until I've read all of Conrad/Melville/Dickens/Austen," or, if the truth be known, the latest Nevada Barr, Elmore Leonard, *Vanity Fair,* or *Comic Relief.* I just love to read, and although my appetite for what Mama referred to as "good, clean trash" has subsided over the past few years, I'm not fastidious.

However, I've come to find out that the works that have survived time's triage are as pleasurable to read as murder mysteries. I was taught that a long time ago, but I feel as though I've only really learned it recently.

In the stone mantelpiece over the fireplace in the library of my college dormitory was carved, "Silent Let Me Sit and Hold High Converse with the Mighty Dead," a fairly off-putting injunction. In college I was the beneficiary of some superlative teaching of literature. The professors were so good that for a while, after I graduated, I didn't see how, unaided, I could fully appreciate a great book. All American high school kids are exposed to them, but my adolescent readings of Jane Austen,

Herman Melville, and George Eliot didn't awaken me to profound interest and pleasure in the novel. It wasn't until Diana O'Hehir's James Joyce seminar and Hunter Hannum's course "The Mind of Modern Germany," in which we read works in translation by Friedrich Nietzsche, Thomas Mann, Franz Kafka, Rainer Maria Rilke, and Hermann Hesse, among others, that literature came fully alive for me and began to matter very much.

Although she was entirely capable of explaining all of Joyce's puns and allusions, Diana O'Hehir approached *Ulysses* as a real novel, not just a mother lode for exegetes. James Joyce changed my life, or the life of my mind; he gave me permission to take inventive liberties with language and to experience interior monologue—that everyday life of an everyman's or -woman's mind—as being as worthy of artistic treatment as the matter of myth. For years thereafter, every solitary walk I took was accompanied by Joyce's kindly hero Leopold Bloom and so was heightened with quotidian symbolism and echoing phrases.

The zenith of the undergraduate literary fest came in my senior year, when as part of an individual study culminating in a thesis on time and transcendence in *Ulysses* and *The Magic Mountain,* Hunter Hannum taught *The Magic Mountain,* lighting his students' way through Mann's masterpiece. The love of literature, in which Hunter and his wife, Hildegarde, continue—there's no trash on their reading tables—became the foundation of a lasting friendship, and the friendship an inspiration to lead the life of the mind.

Still, for years my reading seemed to consist of either needful and often depressing nonfiction or pleasantly numbing good, clean trash. The Eros of literature lay latent until, in 1992, I made that solo journey to India. I decided to take along E. M. Forster's *Passage to India.* I suppose I wanted to dignify my first and very likely only journey to the East, or I may have figured that in the interests of traveling light, a really good book, being demanding, would last me longer than several paperback volumes of brain candy. Reading Forster's sublime story of the impediments to friendship between an English-man and an Indian, and the romance between an English-woman and India itself, was like dining well rather than merely eating. It whetted my appetite for good books. Perhaps by then I had read enough and lived enough and thought enough to be able to savor them well without a mentor.

When I saw the manuscripts displayed in The British Museum on my first visit there, I got choked up. Among them was a copybook containing a draft of *Finnegan's Wake*. With his sight dimming, James Joyce wrote large, in pencil—his phrases and sentences helter-skelter on the left-hand page, revisions in red crayon, and whole new passages scrawled on the right. The handwritten manuscripts of Virginia Woolf's *Mrs. Dalloway*, George Eliot's *Middlemarch*, and Emily Brontë's *Wuthering Heights* were on view, along with John Mil-ton's Commonplace Book and some letters of John Donne. To read a page in the author's own hand, to think of Brontë fair-copying a whole book with a steel pen, and to see that those members of the literary pantheon had struggled with their demon sentences, was to this humanist what the sight of a fragment of the True Cross must be to a devout Catholic.

The gifts of literature are mysterious. The material thing, type on the page, is inert. Those writers' lives were quite likely pinched and cranky, a trial for their nearest and dearest, although there have always been exceptions. Jane Austen was among them, if we can believe the epitaph on her gravestone in Winchester Cathedral. It reads, "In memory of Jane Austen . . . the benevolence of her heart, the sweetness of her temper, and the extraordinary endowments of her mind obtained the

regard of all who knew her and the warmest love of her intimate connections."

Benevolent and sweet, drunken and terrible, or hypochon-
driacal and depressed, many great authors' scrawny remains
have long since gone to dust. Yet their art endures, changing
lives, feeding souls, bringing to mind the good we humans
can do.

8

AUTUMN

To live in a seasonal climate is always to be facing change and often to be carping about it, protesting the revolving discomforts, a little uneasy with the implications of time's passage. It is equally to be confronted by the grand symbolism of the stately turning round of the year. Here, the trees strongly body forth the seasons. In the woods most vividly, every year is an allegory of life's changes. Spring is its infancy, summer its flaming youth, autumn its maturity and fulfillment, winter its ebbing, the end that contains the beginning. It's as foolish to prefer one season above all the rest as it is to hold a preference for a certain time of life. I notice that whatever season we're in is usually my favorite. Perhaps that's an autumnal mind-set.

Although the Sonoran Desert, bioregion of my childhood, is a realm where cacti, not trees, are the charismatic megaflora, Phoenix had watered itself into oasishood, and the yards in our suburb had trees big enough to bond with. The native

saguaros, chollas, ocotillos, mesquites, barrel cacti, and
paloverdes were mostly to be seen on the rapidly receding outskirts of town or in date-palm pastiche desert-style landscapes
at the old Scottsdale and Paradise Valley resorts. The desert
and its cacti were with some justification regarded as hostile;
park-like yards with lawns and elms were the conventional
habitat of Anglo-American families such as mine.

In the yard next door, there were leafy chinaberry trees
where our little gang of kids could clamber into cool shade.
Behind the subdivision was a citrus orchard. With their low,
smooth, elephantine branches, the grapefruit trees were
friendly to small climbers. My family's yard had eucalyptus
trees that were worthless for climbing but impressively tall,
and shading the west side of the house were American elms.
The elms' lowest branches were too high for a little girl to
reach but made a good bandstand for the mockingbirds.

Like any healthy, normal young primate, I became inti-
mately acquainted with trees, if not forests, during my childhood. As most of us do, I outgrew that intimacy. As a young
adult, my feeling for trees persisted but became a rhetorical
relationship. Trees, especially redwoods, along with all the
other conspicuous features of the earth's imperiled ecosystems—sequoias, bristlecone pines, condors, gray whales, snail
darters, Furbish's louseworts—became objects of my general
concern. Before the timber wars got going in earnest, I had left
northern California. Now, courageous acts of civil disobedi-
ence have become a way of life for hundreds of human beings
whose relationship with redwood trees and old-growth forests
goes beyond rhetoric to a sacrifice of their days, their flesh, and
even their lives.

In the mid-1980s, when I moved to the North Woods, I
came to a landscape that had been logged repeatedly and yet
still grew trees. Dwindling tracts of second- and third-growth

hardwoods, mixes of sugar maple, beech, bass, ironwood, ash, poplar, yellow birch, red oak, and hemlock, persist in different combinations and proportions, depending on soil and slope. There are a few white and red pines and white birches here and there, and, near wetlands and flowing water, different forest communities: cedar, fir, spruce, and tamarack. Some ecologists are saying that the combined stresses of acid rain, drought, insects, disease, and the genetic impoverishment that results from cutting the best trees for the market may not be survivable by the forests, despite their current appearance.

Beginning in the mid-nineteenth century, much of this land was cut over and kept cleared. Now it grows corn and hay and golf courses. The uplands are good for growing cherries and other fruit, and for siting half-million-dollar trophy homes with views. Then there's all-but-defeated land such as mine, which was farmed to the limit. In our glacial terrain, the limit was reached after a few crops of potatoes, and the soil began to blow. Now it's parked under pine plantations, where Christmas trees and timber are raised as crops. On my acres, the Christmas trees have been left to their own devices and have grown tall and gnarly, shading and sheltering numerous hopeful cherry, maple, and beech saplings. Our local mosaic of second-, third-, and fourth-growth woodlots, orchards, suburbs, woodburbs, oat fields, and cornfields is picturesque but lacks ecological integrity. None of it adds up to forest, but the robust remnants of the real thing are beautiful for now.

When autumn comes to these woods, the green alchemist chlorophyll, having worked with earth, air, light, and water to grow the trees through spring and summer, ceases its labors. Then every single leaf reveals some different color, pattern, and intensity of pigmentation, going from green to gaudy. There's a spectacle wherever there's a patch of hardwoods. The sugar maple's eye-dazzling range, from plangent yellow to

blazing orange and gleaming ruby, makes that tree's transformations the dominant feature of this most scenic season. After
fifteen years of gaping at the sugar maples' leaves, I have begun
to see past them to the other trees in the forest and their less
insistent but no less beautiful hues. The fall colors of the white
ash's compound leaves grade from butter yellow to garnet and
burgundy, deep radiant tones that quietly invite the eye's
appreciation. Pin cherry leaves are among the earliest to turn
and glow deeply as embers. Hop hornbeams and basswoods
range from chrome yellow to citron. Beech leaves phase
through sunny yellow on their way to paper-bag brown.

The sugar maple's millennia of upstaging the rest of the
fall foliage may be coming to an end. Acid rain threatens these
trees, and global climate change may drive their range northward. Whether the trees themselves will be able to migrate as
quickly as the weather changes remains to be seen. The Asian
longhorn beetle, an alien invasive species recently established
in the United States thanks to the expansion of world trade,
having arrived in the wood of crates containing goods from
China, is likely to infest and decimate this tree species unless
unprecedentedly successful vigilance against the beetle's spread
is undertaken and maintained. The sugar maple's fellow dominant in these woodlands, the American beech, is even more
immediately imperiled. Beech bark disease begins with infestations by a tiny scale insect that open the beeches to invasion
by a fungus that kills the wood. Our conservation district
forester predicts that beech bark disease may eliminate as
many as half of the beech trees. The possibility that the
beeches and sugar maples could all but vanish from the woods,
as did the American chestnuts and elms, which succumbed to
alien organisms, signals change of quite a different kind from
the movement of the seasons and their variation from year to
year. These shocking final changes confront us everywhere

these days, asking insistently, "How are we to live?" and "What are we to do?"

If we live simply, attentively, and gratefully, it will go better. There is always beauty to see if you have an eye for it. Looking is a practice. Seeing is a gift that comes with practice. The light in autumn is so rich, warm, and romantic, tinted with all the bright colors of the land. Did it rejoice the hearts and souls of the old-timers who lived here, engaged in subsistence farming? Were they amazed, grateful? And how did this glowing atmosphere with its rustle and snap strike the Odawa people, when the trees were many and great and the woods offered meat, furs, and medicine and the dangers of wolves and bears? Has it always been a great wonder to be here as the seasons hasten along, and has it always been a vexation to fend with the whipsaw weather that is fall?

There's more to the forest than trees and more to autumn than flamboyant foliage. Autumn has a genius for perfumery. The air wafts of fragrance compounded of the resin of pines and the sweetness of fallen leaves and scores of other scents— dry grasses, horsemint, cornstalks, apples, asters, deer breath, fungus. Weather conducing, the fall fungi are phantasmagorical. One wet November a few years back, my surroundings burgeoned with the fruiting bodies of a wild array of fungi. Slippery Jacks—boletes with slimy caps and spongy undersides—emerged like golden cobbles all along the path between house and studio. Some things that looked like a rubber version of lettuce curled out of the straw mulch on the garden. A host of tiny bird's nest fungi, their perfect little cups seemingly holding three or four white eggs, speckled the front yard's shredded bark. In other places trembled soft taupe parasols unfurling their delicate gills, dainty bodies tumid with all the wetness, seizing the time for scattering their spores and then withering and vanishing. The burly white-and-sulfur amanitas, which had knocked aside clots of moss or lichen to surface and hugely spread their caps, had their moment and passed away. The leathery little bladders of some puffballs remained to issue wisps of dusky spores at the least nudge. Old firewood was frilled with ranks of lurid white up-curling scales.

Autumn is the seed time. Beech trees scatter their mast. Milkweed fluff drifts. The fuzz of goldenrod finds its way forth. Dark little pellets rattle out of the bladderwort capsules. Everyone is sowing haphazardly toward a next generation. There's a luminous felt of panicum grass inflorescences, pressed by the winds against every stopping place. These seed heads are large but light and gangly. When they are ripe, they break away from the leafy bunchgrass clumps and tumble along on their many branches like airy jacks tossed from a wind-child's hand. The seed heads get snatched up in little cyclones and teeter aloft in spirals. On the ground, the stratum of grass seed heads catches the light and makes an aura. More of them catch the wind, whose force prevails, matting them, delicately prickly, against mesh fences and the skirts of the spruce trees that edge the old field. The inflorescences are so agile that they find their way into the house. Some ride in with the firewood, but some, I think, follow the cat in through the two cat flaps to lie shattered, forlorn as fish bones, on the living room floor, adding seasonal interest to the sweepings.

The fungi pervade the soil, going on and on. Some cover vast areas mostly unseen except for their flagrant spore-bearing structures. Perennial grasses can be long-lived, too, sending out their seed stock to sprout somewhere new and then flower, mix, and mingle, acquiring new talents through fertilization come spring. The lives of trees are long and slow and can go on for centuries, even if their autumnal costume changes seem hurried.

When we see those splashes of color appearing around here, we know that the bad sledding weather's almost over. Our thoughts skid from the glories of the hardwood trees' foliage to the pleasing warmth their severed limbs and cut, split trunks can yield in the woodstove. This is the season to be storing up calories, firewood, fruit, nuts, grain—all the fat of the land. It's a brisk time, a time to get busy and prepare for winter. It used to be the reaping, threshing, canning, and slaughtering time. Now it's become another occasion to summon the tourists to see the fall color, to sell them souvenirs at a scatter of homely crafts festivals; to tempt the upscale custom with trendy edibles at aspiring wineries and bakeries, with arty extravagances at galleries and boutiques.

Deer hunting remains an unbroken if sorely frayed thread of connection with the timeless tasks of autumn. The hunt begins in September and is restricted to hunters using black powder in muzzle-loading guns. Next, bow hunting is permitted. Hunting season reaches its bloody climax in mid-November, when rifles are the weapons allowed. In principle I have no objection to hunting the white-tailed deer. Their superabundant numbers may be attributed to changes in the land, clearance that opened up so much browse, and to wildlife management policies that encourage their proliferation if not their health. The deer are bountiful prey and have long been good meat, magical American beings. Hunting is as elemental as cellular life, and pitiless. We have extirpated the animals that preyed on us and on the deer, so it falls to humanity to cull and to kill.

Commercialism and technology make boorishness all but inescapable in this relationship to the wild. Composite bows, portable stands for perching in trees to await the deer, piles of bait—corn, apples, carrots, sugar beets—high-powered rifles, ammunition and sights, blaze orange coveralls, four-wheelers, and oceans of beer and schnapps are the accoutrements of hunting nowadays. Many thousands of aspiring Nimrods flock north every fall, and their beer purchases seem to be a mainstay of the tourist economy. Incidents of armed, inebriated strangers taking dead aim at the slightest motion and killing dogs, cows, cousins, and women hanging out the wash have tarnished the sport's image.

Still, I have careful friends who hunt for the satisfaction and economy of putting food on the table, and although I'm sure that I lack the nerve to kill another big animal or even to dispatch a small, injured bird, getting meat by hunting seems more honorable to me than just shopping for it. I invite my neighbor from across the road to hunt out back on my land, and not disinterestedly. If he gets a deer, I'll get some venison. He's been generous in sharing his kill.

During hunting season, the butchers in all the small towns around here work late into the night, dressing deer by skinning them. Out behind the famous Polish charcuterie in Pineville one November day, I noticed a deer head and hide, complete, in the back of a pickup truck. The flesh and bones were elsewhere, the venison by now packaged and freezing in white paper, yet the dead deer's eyes were open and glistened beneath a modest crown of antlers. The skin looked soft as a robe. For a second, the deer's regalia called for a sorcerer to don them and dance, and for the dance to be fixed in soot and ochre, to work life magic on a deep cave wall.

Writing in the house this evening, I'm watching a little old knot of wood, riddled by fungus and insects, burn in the woodstove. It makes just a small fire, all I need to keep the chill off. The longing to draw near a domesticated fire at nightfall is probably *Homo sapiens'* fourth great craving, after thirst, hunger, and lust. Burning wood, watching flames, and getting warm are older than archaic.

Zen practitioners, in their wisdom of simplicity, say, "Chop wood, carry water," but my work begins where the woodcutter's leaves off. Tending the woodstove is the central discipline of half the year, relieved occasionally by car trips, jet trips, phone calls, and the easy electric heat out in the studio. Personally or by proxy, I burn many different kinds of fuel, from fossil to forest. Some implicate me in acid rain, some in smog, and all, even the wood, in global warming. Of the several fuels I use, though, wood's combustion produces the least carbon dioxide pound for pound. Cutting down those trees to burn them, however, eliminates a carbon sink. Plants, especially the old and slow-growing, sequester carbon.

If reducing my contribution to the greenhouse effect were my paramount motivation, I would run my home on wind and solar power and extreme conservation measures. To live off the grid just takes some forethought, a front-end investment in the apparatus, and the willingness to learn the mechanics of homestead-scale appropriate technologies. When they malfunction, there's no power company to call if the lights go off and the pump quits. The utility is you.

In some places, ratepayers can now exercise a preference for renewable energy. Ecological designers, energy mavens, and intermediate technologists tell us a comfortable life can be sustained without the devastation that the extraction, combustion, generation, and transmission of nonrenewable energy now wreak. Clearly, the current infrastructure needs a little more work before that middle way is achieved, and some locales are taking it upon themselves to do that work. Hopeful evidence of this trend stands in a cornfield a dozen miles east of my home. It's a huge, gleaming white wind generator erected a few years ago by a municipally owned utility. The windmill was capitalized by a number of utility customers who were willing to pay a "green rate," a slightly higher but fixed price for clean, atmosphere-friendly electricity. Apparently those ratepayers thought they *could* do something about the weather. Meanwhile, all around me are houses that are off the grid, making their own energy and not freezing in the dark. Homes such as these are no longer exotic and offer good shelter as the winds of change begin to howl.

Unfortunately, the utility that serves my neck of the woods isn't dispensing renewable energy. Inertia, disinclination to plan, and an aversion to reading instruction manuals keep me wired into the grid for illumination and for water pumping. I purchase propane for cooking and for running the fridge and water heater. Aesthetics keeps me heating with wood. It's a messy, toilsome habit, but the warmth of the stove and sight of the flames are earned pleasures, not assumed amenities.

Some autumns are more riotous than others. Some slouch past dully. Some announce themselves with the rude crack of a killing frost. They all raise the question, "What kind of winter must I prepare for, and how does the best guess translate into cords of firewood?" Standing in my living room on an early August afternoon, relaxed in the vague heat within the shady house and lapped by sedate breezes, I may look at the woodstove and realize that the first fall fire to warm that hearth may be needed soon. What if this winter is harsher than the last? What if we get the long, cold, snowy winter I always pray for? If by September I haven't bought my firewood and begun splitting and stacking it, the nuisance quotient of that besought winter will treble.

Although in these parts wood splitting is a commonplace, it's still a kind of novelty to me. Whenever I talk to city-dwelling friends, I try to work wood splitting into the conversation. I've even considered trying to deduct the cost of my firewood as a research expense on the grounds that a writer is always working, and here I am, writing about firewood. (Actually, we do get a home heating tax credit that applies to the cost of firewood as well as other kinds of fuel and energy.)

The wood I buy is a by-product of county road "improvement." The trees are felled and cut into stove lengths with a chain saw, machine-split with a piston, and loaded into a truck, and then two or three truckloads are hauled to my home, where they are unloaded. Thoreau remarked that the wood warms you more than once. I count at least four times—felling, splitting, loading, and unloading—that my purchasing spares me.

Stacked wood is the handiest. Therefore, my largest opportunity to get preheated by my firewood is in attending to that chore. In order to form the ricks, I usually plant some steel fence posts to support the ends. Because I do this only once a year, if then, obtaining a sledgehammer, mallet, or fence-post driver that would sit idle for 364 days of the year doesn't occur to me until I once again employ the blunt end of my splitting maul to drive the fence posts into the ground. Because the stakes start out at shoulder height, the maul's long handle, whose leverage is perfect for leading the heavy steel wedge on a long arc through a chunk of wood, becomes a major nuisance in the fence-post hammering. At some point in this job, I usually wind up just taking the gleaming metal head in my gloved hands and awkwardly banging away at the T-shaped end of the fence post, aware that the only advantage of this over using a rock is that the steel is less apt to shatter. The fence-post banging, however, evokes the long span of human experience during which rocks, sticks, and bones were all the tools there were, and all the repetitive, strenuous, mesmerizing movements entailed in the use of primal tools.

A wood-splitting maul is a very basic technology from a lineage that goes back to the dawn of our kind. *Homo sapiens'* invention of the ax remade—or unmade—the world. Here, about a century ago, the ax and the two-man saws known as "misery whips" effected the Big Cut of the North Woods. This rapid deforestation by hand is, in its way, as much a wonder of the world as the pyramids for volume of sweat, and perhaps more so in terms of the magnitude of its effect on nature and culture.

A steel ax head or maul mass-produced is a small but undeniable link to iron and coal mines, blast furnaces, and all the exploitations and pollutions that go with them. Maul in hand, confronting a big length of stove wood that could serve as a cold winter night's log, and splitting it into several sticks suitable for making light, brief fires on cool fall or spring evenings, is real work and highly gratifying. The pieces of wood excerpt the life stories of many trees, every fragment telling of a tree's seasons of growth, its branchings, twistings, and strength or weakness. Each piece of wood split has an inner beauty. The maul opens diptychs composed of wood insect galleries, grain, hue, and stain of rot. A piece ruffled with white shelf fungus along every fissure in its orderly bark, shot through with mycelia, light as balsa, may be poor in BTUs but great fuel for reflection on the power of beings as simple as fungi to consume, transform, and embellish the world.

Dealing with firewood gets me out-of-doors and breathing, sometimes gasping, fresh air in the cold weather. It's a big chore to split and stack the eight or twelve cords of stove wood I purchase annually. I don't usually complete it without help, but the more wood wrangling I do myself, the more boasting I can do. Splitting wood is a lot more fun than stacking it. The fact is that whether or not it's neatly stacked, the wood is still flammable. Not to get the firewood stacked and covered before the snow flies is feckless. Then wood fetching becomes wood mining, tunneling through the snow.

The Latin for *hearth* is *focus*, the spot whence rays of heat and light emanate. A place to draw near and warm the bones makes a good focus. Making a fire in the woodstove requires a sufficiency of time. The heat takes a while. In the meantime, there's an opportunity to defer gratification. It's also possible to hurry through the chore of fire making, although not to hurry the fire, and to gripe unphilosophically about every step of the process.

Using a woodstove means that the temperature within the house varies widely, as with the temperature outside. Throughout fall, winter, and spring, the nights are cold and the fire wanes. The house cools down and grows chilly as I sleep. The hope is that the stove will hold enough coals that the place won't be stone-cold in the morning and there will be some embers to kindle the new day's fire. In the bitterest cold weather, when the wind is blowing, I just keep feeding the woodstove like a stoker in the boiler room, never completely dispelling the chill but keeping the pipes from freezing, at least. I wake myself in the middle of the night to feed the fire, even though the bed is the spot I never want to leave.

There's the warmth I want and the warmth I don't. When it's cold, I want warmth in my house, and I burn wood to obtain it. As a result, I'm contributing to the greenhouse effect and so to the warmth I don't want. Even the oil industry is no longer monolithically disputing the reality of global climate change, but the rest of the world has been waiting for the fossil-fueled American Way of Life to come up for discussion ever since George Bush tabled the subject at the 1992 United Nations Conference on Environment and Development in Rio de Janeiro. U.S. heel-dragging continued at international treaty conferences on climate change in Kyoto and in the Hague in the early 2000s.

In the summer of 2000, our local daily newspaper published, albeit far from the front page, a wire service story on the release of *Climate Change in America—A Report to Congress*. The story forecast that "entire ecosystems may shift northward as temperatures increase. . . . Sugar maples could disappear from northeastern forests. . . . The Great Lakes are predicted to decline because of increased evaporation," and "in much of America, winter may disappear."

I, for one, would miss winter. I had an experience of endless summer during my early years in Phoenix, and it was a hot kind of dull. Still, there are the indefatigable optimists who see nothing ominous in being able to golf here in late November in their shirtsleeves.

Failing incorrigible optimism, one might achieve some detachment from the terrible implications of global climate change by resorting to science or cosmology or a fine blend of the two. As has been learned by paleoecologists, who take the longer view, and ecological restorationists, who work to rehabilitate ecosystems that depend for their health on periodic floods and fires, the earth can make a creative response to disturbance. Tornadoes, hurricanes, lightning-set wildfires, rock slides, glaciations, earthquakes, avalanches, volcanoes, floods, and storms that remodel coastlines are natural and need not be considered disasters.

Evolution came up with suites of organisms capable of revegetating and reinhabiting all kinds of blasted terrains. Before the ecosphere became real estate and before we roaming troops of primates adopted fixed residences, got fruitful, and multiplied into the billions, what we now call natural disasters were neither tragic nor devastating. They exacted their toll in lives yet left swaths of renewal in their wake, patches where the succession of plants and animals could start over and vary the landscape, making resilience through diversity. Of course, the reinhabitation depended on there being refugia, undisturbed populations of likely plants and animals, connected to places where the new settlers could exist. After the disturbance ceased, new seeds and spiders, shrubs and snakes could filter in, by waves or wind or animal locomotion, and begin to be an ecosystem again. Of course, the recovery from natural disturbance could require anywhere from a few years to several millennia. Upheavals of sufficient magnitude could cause local extinctions. Once in a while, an asteroid would hit the planet and the extinctions would be more than local—adios, dinosaurs.

The more sanguine, scientific big-picture types rightly observe that the earth can abide big change, even change as big as global warming. It's all in an epoch's work, but in the long run, as the economist John Maynard Keynes observed, we are all dead. So perhaps it's a mistake to get in a flap over this vast planetary disturbance with climate change, extinctions, and ecosystem collapses exacerbating one another, and all of them largely attributable to *Homo sapiens*. Ever since sexual reproduction began on the planet 1,500 million years ago, when microorganisms with nuclei in their cells stumbled into the practice of going halfsies and shuffling hereditary traits and death evolved, life and death for all of us save the bacteria have been inseparable. We chickens are just the egg's way of making another egg.

Hinduism presents worshipers with a sublime and terrifying divinity, Kali, who embodies the ineluctable fact of the world-renewing sacrifice. "She represents the cyclical time consciousness that transcends individual destiny," explains Ajit Mookerjee in *Kali: The Feminine Force*. "Kali . . . in her 'forceful' role is the antagonist of all evil in the eternal cosmic struggle, yet she is herself the personification of all benign and terrible forces." She's a bloodthirsty old gal dancing with her lei of fifty severed heads and her girdle of human hands, standing on or straddling Shiva's supine form out at the cremation grounds. Floods, fires, and pestilence, says Kali—who is, like Shiva, sometimes represented as dancing in a purificatory circle of flames—are just the way this endlessly unstatic cosmos works and turns. Thus has one great and multifarious religion personified and venerated the entwining of generation and destruction. Mother Kali dances to the necessity and promise of wildfires, the charnel house, the cemetery, and the compost heap, along with inordinate numbers of carrion beetles, all manner and means of endings and transformations of razing the dead and returning them to wider circulation.

Through no deficiency on the part of Mother Kali or Mother Nature, I haven't arrived at any cosmic equanimity concerning the destruction of the current planetary ecosystem, let alone of my person or my household. I can't picture a North Woods without sugar maples and beeches, and the increasingly likely prospect of purificatory flames having their way with the moribund trees in our besieged forests prompts thoughts of fleeing, not jigging like the great goddess in a ring of fire.

As with warmth, there's the fire I want and the fire I don't. My house is surrounded by pine trees, a very flammable tribe. To live hemmed in by conifers is ill-advised, but the trees were here before me, and so I mostly leave them to be, especially because they hide me from the world's gaze and vice versa. I'm a privacy-loving aesthete; maybe someday I'll be an immolated aesthete. The fire I do want needs to be kept strictly inside the woodstove and nowhere else on the property. Given the years of low rainfall and the fact of low soil moisture, the general warming, and a load of fuel in the form of branches, needles, and dead trees on the ground, the fire I don't want may be what I get.

Thanks to the writings of Norman Maclean, whose *Young*

Men and Fire details the true story of thirteen valiant smoke jumpers who died in Montana fighting the Mann Gulch fire in 1949, and to the works of fire historian Stephen J. Pyne (*Fire in America* and *World Fire*), I am too well supplied with horrific images of wildfire blowups and forest firestorms. Through the 1870s and into the early 1900s, huge swaths of the upper Midwest were burned bare in some places by great fires feeding on the slash left behind after the logging era. The Peshtigo fire in Wisconsin killed perhaps 1,500 people. The 1908 Metz, Michigan, fire burned more than 2.3 million acres. Descriptions of these mass fires called the word *firestorm* into existence. Many of these holocausts were started naively, lit by farmers persuaded that firing the slash would prepare the soil as well as clear the land for agriculture. Long before homesteads and cabins in the woods came equipped with gas-fired barbecue grills, propane tanks, natural gas lines, shake roofs, and heating oil reservoirs, wildfire ignited by human deeds had its way around here.

More than once during the hot, droughty summers of the 1990s, the post office doors in Tamarack City and Pineville bore notices of the governor's proclamation of an "extreme fire emergency" all across the region. Although it was good that the public was being alerted to the danger, the sight of these little posters wasn't reassuring. How would a few paragraphs of fine print deter some carefree vacationer from flinging a burning cigarette out the car window as he sped along the state highway a mile south of my house, headed for the lakeshore, or discourage weekend campers from lighting their one campfire of the year and torching the countryside with a stray flaming marshmallow?

If, instead of worrying what others might do, I seriously wanted to reduce the threat of wildfire on my premises, I could follow some fire department rules of thumb by clearing and mowing a thirty-foot perimeter around my house and thinning and limbing the trees fifty yards beyond that. How this might be accomplished in the spare time of a daydreaming, chain saw–less tree-hugger is as hard for me to imagine as living on a denuded lot exposed to public view.

Although I continue to hope that the flames will give me a pass, a few years ago I did thin out the pines and clear up some of the tinder and kindling immediately around the house. With the help of an able young couple, I accomplished some controlled destruction that was nothing like the radical deforestation real fire safety would require.

Since the age of twelve, Jason had been getting the family firewood with a bow saw. He knew how to cut down a tree. Denise, his wife, was looking for work in landscaping. Singly and together, they were willing to spend some hours every day for a few weeks cutting, trimming, and grinding up Scotch pine trees. Jason wielded his chain saw with marvelous accuracy, able to drop a tree right where he wanted it to go.

Because the whole point of the endeavor was to reduce the fire hazard, we could neither burn the trees nor leave them to dry, so I rented a chipper, a truly frightening machine capable of devouring whole a pine tree as much as a foot in diameter and fifteen feet tall and spitting it out as a pile of two- or three-inch wood chips. This machine seemed to be the only practical way to dispose of the trees once they were down. I had no immediate use for them, although stripped they might have served as fence posts.

We parked the chipper in the driveway. Rather than moving the machine to the trees and leaving ruts and other damage in our path, we dragged the trees cut from the surrounding few acres to it. Even with the infernal machine, this was a labor-intensive project and had its dangers. The deafening whining and grinding of the chipper made me feel a panicked

urgency. One slip and the lives and limbs of more than pine
trees could be forfeit. After several trees had been cut and
hauled to the chipper, I would use a pitchfork to feed twigs
and branches into the machine's maw, trying to find a rhythm
with Jason, who fed in large limbs and whole trees by turn.

Later, as I worked alone, clambering on stacks of Scotch
pines, I thought of the dreadful risks the lumberjacks faced,
such as when someone had to pick his way down the thousands of logs caught and backed up in a river and then prise
apart and unleash the logjam. That whole world would have
had the sharp, clean reek of pine resin, as mine did during that
few-days-long logging era.

Jason and Denise did a ferocious amount of hard, heavy
work. Part of the time, I worked alongside them and took my
beating, getting whipped by limbs as a main stem headed into
the chipper or struck in the forehead by a wood chip shot five
yards out of the machine. I wound up generally cut and
bruised and stumbling with fatigue. The more I tired, the less
useful and the more hazardous I became to my co-workers.
Jason seemed always to be alert no matter what, which is the
only way to be when you're working with something as monstrous as a chipper or tricky as a chain saw on uncertain foot-
ing among limbs and around trees that have been cut and are
falling.

Even though pines are softwood and stove wood is hard, I
got a better understanding of the work of wood cutting. I
began to see how much intelligence of the body and determination of the mind are required. Mindless muscle would just
get one ground up or crushed. Does being accustomed to the
work make the aches any less at the end of the day? How much
difference would it have made if I were in my twenties, like
Jason and Denise? Leon Murphy, from whom I buy my firewood, is in his sixties. Wood selling is his after-hours job.

Every year, he gets up about 300 cords. A cord is about a four-by-four-by-eight stack of wood representing enormous labor, whose value is no mere theory.

Besides fire safety, I had another purpose in thinning the pines around my house. I wanted to begin to make good my pledge to do some restoration on my land. This place grew hardwoods and still does. Everywhere under the pines are maple and beech seedlings biding their time. Sometimes on my strolls I take along my work gloves, clippers, and loppers and go about uprooting Scotch pine seedlings or cutting them off at the ground. The idea is to reduce the competition that the pines pose to the returning hardwoods.

Another restoration activity, and one I much prefer, is planting trees. When I'm out prowling through my bocage and encounter one of the oaks that I've planted randomly over the years, it's a happy surprise. Oaks are slow, but they are dogged. Of all the broad-leaved seedlings I have stuck in my coniferous acres—including such species as hemlock, likelier than the oaks to have been found in this particular place—few, if any, appear to have taken hold or survived the rodent and deer appetites for vegetation. Red and white oak seedlings and acorns poked in the sand seem to like it here. In the fall, I'll spot their clusters of outsized leaves, still low to the ground, turning scarlet or tan and looking as if they plan to endure.

Trees, the timber interests tell us, are a renewable resource. There's some truth to that. It is possible, through industrial forestry, to clear-cut and replant fast-growing varieties of conifers in quick rotation and get a yield of wood fiber from the land repeatedly, but not indefinitely. Other, more conservative, foresters suggest that 1 percent of the trees in a forest be the maximum annual harvest. A hundred-year rotation is closer to the natural rhythm of a community of trees. Several years back, I visited Aldo Leopold's Sand County farm and saw with my own eyes the pines that have been growing tall since the dust bowl days, when the Leopold family spent weekends planting pines by the hundreds and eventually thousands. It is indeed possible to replant trees and have them grow, but there's far more to a forest than a handful of tree species. Whether real forests can be reestablished on my acreage under the present circumstances is doubtful, but it is a doubt I try to deflect.

In my talks, I try to kindle some hope and a renewed sense of possibility. I have to hope that humanity's ravishment of the wild and wooded ground of our being need not beget an entirely artifactual world. My fervent prayer is that somehow we can save the wild remaining, preserve it, restore it, expand it, and someday return to our give-and-take with it.

Late one winter, in a keynote talk to a conference of individuals and groups interested in preserving, enhancing, and restoring natural areas in the parks of Toronto—a few dozen working stewards, volunteers, and park employees—I tried to conjure for them a vision of the primal Carolinian forest that had grown in their area. I spoke of rivers teeming with salmon, of wooded creeks, and of the many kinds of life that might be restored there through their continuing dedication, hope and study, hard work, and good teaching—and a whole lot of miracles.

Most of those listening seemed to be interested and inspired by such images and were, I hope, heartened. Afterward, however, a young forester asked me whether I really thought it wise or fair to encourage people to strive for outcomes so fantastic. She wasn't a cynic, and it wasn't a trick question—it was posed by a mother who, when she wasn't paying professional attention to the Metro Park woodlands, was trying honestly to envision a future for her daughter, trying to judge what would be the best she could hope for rather than blindly hoping for the best. All I could offer was my respect for her courage and the thought that we need to be working for the optimum.

Her good, if hellish, question is related to the question of how we are to live in the world civilization has unmade. What are we to do with our knowledge of and ongoing participation in that unmaking?

Those are personal questions. How am I going to live as the diversity of the forest dwindles, if the spring falls silent and the fall has no scarlet? The question behind that question is this: When do we abandon the effort to maintain some semblance of our primal landscapes? When do we forgo the hope of ecosystem health? When do we, or I, quit working and caring for nature?

The answer within me varies with the time of day, with the cloud cover, with my location, indoors or out. Back home from Toronto a little later in the year, I strolled out back one afternoon, pondering how to live and what to hope for. The answer came that we live by being grateful for what there is. If the Asian longhorn beetle does in the sugar maple, we'll turn to the red maple. If the gypsy moth or oak wilt finishes off the oaks, we'll enjoy the pines, even the Scotch pines. If air pollution, soil depletion, excess nitrogen, and ultraviolet radiation make all the trees weak and susceptible to bugs and fungi and bacteria and the trees don't survive, then if any of us survive, we'll admire the beauty of the lichens and the grasses, and we'll keep trying to grow trees and restore natural forests as long as we live, as long as we can, as long as anyone around remembers how and why. We may look to the squirrels and jays, to the winds and waters, for help in this. Human will and human work are not the only strong forces on the planet.

9

WINTER

In 1998 the winter was truly pagan, for it began in good earnest right at the solstice, with plenty of snow, cold winds blowing, and temperatures below freezing. How apt it is that ancient custom here in the Northern Hemisphere holds that the year begins with the return of the light, even though it's the onset of winter. The days do grow longer, but the season is a challenge.

Long past dusk on that longest night of the year, I was driving some thirty miles to an annual solstice gathering at a bed and breakfast–cum–peace and ecology center that functions as a focal point of the local counterculture.

All day, the radio meteorologists had been making their usual prejudicial remarks about the imminent weather, posting a "winter storm warning." It sounds bad, and indeed it can be. Caution is warranted, especially if one is foolhardy enough to be out on the road. That night, there was so much snow howling down that I couldn't see anything in my headlights but the whirl of white feathers in a sea of pitch-black. That snow accumulated so quickly that the road itself disappeared, its margins effaced. Forewarned, I made the grueling, chancy drive, following the tracks of the car ahead and hoping its destination might be the same as mine. No wonder we love our cars. I sat in mine warm and toasty, traveling in weather that could have killed me if I'd had to make the journey by simpler means. I was able to join with a score of friends in candlelit prayers and wishes for peace in the coming year and then return to my house and sleep in my own bed.

Next morning, back at home, I could see that the time had come to limber up the Sorel boots, those heavy, waterproof snow boots so indispensable to life in this wintery clime. Once again, it was time to remember how to be cold gracefully. There's a limit finally to what artifice can accomplish in mitigating the effects of this severe force of nature. There would be no going barefoot, even inside the house, for a while, and out in the writing studio, despite the straw bales placed around its base for insulation and the fact that the little electric heater was turned up full blast, on some days it just wouldn't warm up. I sit at my desk stiff and crabbed, braced against the chill, preoccupied by the cold. My thoughts center on the question of how to get warmer. How many layers of clothing could I bundle myself in before losing all mobility? Fingerless gloves help. Would it be cheating, I wonder, to wear a hat indoors?

Writing barely qualifies as activity. The moving finger doesn't move enough to bestir heat in the hand, much less in the toes. The blood goes gelid as the water in the cat's dish. It's really a wonder that there was any literature produced in the so-called temperate zone prior to central heating. Then, to be a writer, or any other kind of poor, was usually to be cold in winter. Heating the garret cost money. The bohemian's choice might have been between coal in the grate or a loaf on the table. At the moment, cheap electricity keeps my work space workable and me working. If the price shot up or the grid went down, could I muster the fortitude to keep writing?

Snow is a discipline and solitude is a discipline. The cynics say to be careful what you pray for because you may get it. Around the autumnal equinox, I begin to long for it to snow and to keep snowing, from winter solstice to vernal equinox. The image is of keeping to myself, sleeping and eating, reading and writing, thinking and skiing in the pristine white preserve of home.

Of course, the longing imagination is wont to edit out the annoying details, such as the daily mess that comes with wood heat. The trek out to the woodpile and back tracks in clots of snow. With the armloads of stove wood come chunks of bark and other organic matter that acquire dirt status upon entry to the house. Cleaning the ash out of the woodstove stirs up a cloud of fine gray particles that sift down to coat every surface, including my lungs.

Imagination omits the fact that on some winter days, making myself get out from under the heap of body-warmed bedcovers and moving around in the cold seems as challenging as mounting a polar expedition. Eventually the call of nature, from within or from without, as sounded by Simone the cat, can no longer be balked, and so the day begins. After rekindling the fire in the woodstove, I fill the sink with dirty dishes and then add hot water and let them soak. That way, the water that's been imbibing chemicals in the plastic plumbing overnight can be cleared and put to some use. Then I can fill the kettle and put it on to boil for tea, and then get some more water salted and boiling in a saucepan for oatmeal. Breakfast gets made at random, along with moments of cat play, house tidying, face washing, bed making, and layering up to greet the day.

During the fall, when I'm dreaming of a white solstice, I forget about the flinching from the cold and the trussed feeling that accessorizes appropriate winter attire. As winter consolidates its rule and deepens the cold a little every day, my summer-bared limbs disappear under successive layers of clothing, there to blanch for months before once again experiencing the sun. The improbable choice of naked apes to live year-round in a seasonal climate was contingent on the technological advance we know as clothing. Long underwear is surrogate fur, offering the warmth without the allure. This and other innovations—such as woolen coats and trousers—permit more agility than the once-prized buffalo robe. Long johns undermine gender stereotyping and make an antifashion statement. My lumpy January ensemble is a world away from the sometimes swanky getups I wore around San Francisco. Even locally, in contrast to the youthful miniskirted nymphs and T-shirt-wearing skateboarders who are out and about downtown in the cold weather, I am dressed for no success, at least not in flirting. In the town or in the country, warm in my turtlenecks, wool sweaters, and socks, wearing several layers of clothing altogether, I am clad for comfort and not for speed.

When the snowy winter of my dreams occurs in reality, it requires constant shoveling. Keeping the pathways open down to the ash heap, out to the bird feeder, around the woodpile, over to the compost heap, and to the studio beyond becomes a substantial project. If it's at all windy, shoveling snow can be an extremely brisk outing. By the time I'm fully costumed for the chore in an outfit that's been accreting over the years, I look as if Mars were my next destination. First, I don a neoprene face mask, which makes me look like the villain in a teen slasher movie or a down-on-his luck starship trooper from a third-rate galaxy, but keeps my cheeks from being raddled by the cold. Then come the neck scarf, windbreaker, toque, boots, gloves, and mittens. Thus attired, I can be a shoveling fool, even work up a sweat, even though it may be nine degrees and blowing outside.

I'm competent in shoveling snow. It would be stretching it to claim that I enjoy it, but I've convinced myself that it's good for me. I'm unlikely to be any tougher than necessary. Fortitude is a cardinal virtue, though, so I have made some choices that exact it. By forgoing the assistance of a gas-powered snowblower, I've purchased some strength and a blessed silence. Not wishing to make a career out of shoveling snow, however, I hire someone to plow my driveway clear. How strong do I really need to be?

Shoveling snow, like dishwashing and unlike writing, quickly produces evidence of work done. The results, however, are as transient as clean dishes, and the task is almost as Sisyphean. Successive snows find me digging out my paths again and again. I figure I'm in training to turn out like some of the old women legendary around here—people's widowed grandmothers or aunts who just stayed on their farms and walked to church on Sundays. Without benefit of mates or internal combustion engines, they managed well within their modest means and lived on beyond their eighties.

Maybe their secret was not expecting comfort. My consumer-class generation and those following have been so misled by this bizarre and singular historical episode of fossil fuel use that lacking a dishwasher can count as a social grievance and year-round climate control is taken as normal.

At the dawn of the twenty-first century, however, year-round climate change is a fait accompli. Anecdotal evidence abounds, and the scientific consensus is firm. In the decade and a half I've lived here, our winters have become warmer, drier, and shorter. My midlife infatuation with snow may not be a lasting romance unless I'm willing to migrate northward with the cold. Even there, the polar sea ice is melting rapidly. Alaskan permafrost is thawing, and shrubbery is invading the tundra.

Whatever the reasons, a serious weeklong winter storm with a few feet of snow accumulation has become a rare event. When such a storm hits, it changes everything. The pines are clabbered with snow. The churning air is opaque with snow. Snow coats everything, drifts and sifts into shoveled paths, fills them and makes them disappear, buries the roads, halts the world. Weatherpersons warn us against blowing and drifting snow and severe wind chills. In loco parentis, they tell us to bundle up; we're under house arrest from natural causes.

A good snowfall is both confining and protective. The confinement is straightforward enough. Driving for any but the most urgent purpose is purely crazy. Going out at all, completely bundled, still invites the cold into your bones, exhausts you, and saps your wits. Leaving the woodstove unfed for even an hour allows the house to chill, and the warmth seems harder to retrieve. In a setup like mine, someone's got to keep the home fires burning—and that someone is me.

Snow's protection is also a function of the difficulty it causes. For one thing, miscreants, most of whom are on the lazy side, are unlikely to make mischief in harsh conditions. What if the getaway car won't start? Then there's the tracking factor to consider. When the wind dies down, every footstep on the snow, even that of a mouse, leaves its mark.

With an overcast sky in a storm's aftermath, snow light is lurid, luminous, and strange, as though the snow has captured light from above the clouds and borne it to earth. When the new-fallen snow is fluffy and plentiful, the departure of a chickadee from a pine branch is physics enough to dislodge a white dab and cause it to disassociate into trailing powdery skeins, to fall again and finally reach the ground. On and on it can go, this continuous cold tumbling of crystals from clouds, precipitating a hush on the land.

The occasional abysmally cold day simplifies everything: Warmth is all that matters. In the introduction to his translation of Lucretius' *The Nature of Things*, Frank O. Copley comments that "the symbol of epicurean pleasure is the 'picnic,' a group of relaxed, untroubled people sitting on the soft grass in the shade of a tree near a running stream, enjoying the mere aspect of nature and caring for their creature needs with the simplest of food and drink."

How to reconcile Stephanie of the North with Epicurus? As I dig my way through the trackless white wastes out to the studio, there are cold, stung cheeks, stinging fingertips, and the aches that follow on lifting shovelful after shovelful of sometimes heavy snow. Pain is not absent from the experience.

More pertinent might be Friedrich Nietzsche's "That which does not destroy me makes me stronger." Epicurus, thought Nietzsche, was decadent. Biogeography may not be completely irrelevant to this philosophical difference. A picnic in your chiton by some creek in Athens could be a daily proposition, whereas Nietzsche, in Basel, probably couldn't have been much of a lounger.

Shoveling snow does avail one of winter's keener pleasures. It is good just to be outside, watching the land's voluptuous white mantle forming and reforming itself, pausing to catch my breath, and hearing the mild sounds that affirm the stillness—the wind moving softly through the heavy-laden pine boughs, the squeaky exchange of chickadee greetings.

If it is achieved in the six days ahead of Sunday, deep snow makes for a true Sabbath. On Sunday, the motorized din of getting and spending abates. No gravel trucks ply the nearby highway. Automobile traffic is minimal. If said Sunday includes some choice televised football, the snowmobilers, whose fun rapes the quiet, may stay inside to watch the game, thus keeping the Sabbath holy. If such a Sabbath happens not to see a snowfall and there's no call for shoveling, then the North Woods equivalent of an epicurean picnic awaits. I can enjoy the mere aspect of nature on my cross-country skis.

It may yet be quite cold, but when after a run of dim gray days, blue sky appears, the sunlight incites a riot of color in the formerly monochrome landscape—cerulean sky and cobalt shadow, viridian pines, silvery maple bark, umber cherry trunks, ochre beech leaves—and Earth, sweet magic maker, is full of glory. When the new year's sun gleams, glares, ricochets, and charges the air with light that infuses the very snow on the ground, the magic is finished in beauty.

Before setting out on one such dazzling day, I darned a hole in the fingertip of one of the gloves I would wear under my mittens and then dressed to go skiing in a total of fifteen items of clothing, counting pairs as one. The underlying cross-country ski outfit is whatever I'm wearing that day. It's a cheap and simple sport. All one needs in order to have a good time is skis, boots, and poles.

In 1984, Phil, a native who knew that the best way to get through the winter is to get out and play in it, gave me a set of cross-country skis for my birthday. Owing to that automobile accident, six years elapsed between my opening the comically outsized gift-wrapped box containing the skis and my first outing on them.

Whenever I do something like skiing that requires two fully functioning, roughly equal and responsive legs, I feel another round of gratitude to everyone who abetted my recovery. There was the humane, quirky, perfectionist orthopedic surgeon. There was the vegetarian angel who was willing to bring me a steak she'd cooked to perfection when, from the hospital bed, my body cried out for good meat. Through the skill and kindness of many such agents of healing, I regained my mobility and some zest for using it. Thus, at forty-two I was able to figure out the basics of cross-country skiing and develop such an enthusiasm for it that I recently wore out that first pair of skis. At the turn of the millennium, Dad's Christmas money bought me a new set.

Qualifying my sense of the virtuous frugality of my non-motorized winter sport of choice was the realization that these gleaming new skis weren't exactly made of hemp by a lesbian cooperative. They're the latest thing in ski technology. I shudder to think how toxic the resins used in them may be and how underpaid the workers who assembled the boots. My diversions, too, demand their pound of earth flesh. One other item pertinent to my simple winter pleasures is the thirty-five acres of land belonging to me. With the permission of my neighbors to venture onto their forty, and weather permitting, I can just about ski out my back door and travel half a mile without leaving home. If the sun is out and the snow is at all passable, it would be a sin against pleasure not to go. Being free to act spontaneously when such moments present themselves is a wealth greater than a sultan's cave of jewels.

Sometimes, as in those months that followed my mother's death, that freedom and this place just seem necessary for survival. That first winter after Mama died, I mourned constantly, indoors and out, moving and sitting still. I wish I could say that my relationship with my mother was wonderful, but that was not the case. Be that as it may, our tie was the greatest power in my life. The grief at its fleshly ending has been great also.

That winter's beauties of cold and calm, of twigs and branches coruscating with sequins of frost, of glittering, breeze-smoothed snow and spangly showers of diamond dust dislodged by some small force—a squirrel's sigh, a chickadee's shiver—were both consolation and knives in the heart. Over and over, I had to realize that I couldn't share those beauties with my mother.

My mother loved nature and was especially interested in birds, but she was readily captivated by the doings of any of the small animals that chanced into our suburban life. Over the years, mouse and bird rescues contributed to the family's body of animal stories. Occasional bird rarities, such as the bittern attracted to the lily-pool oasis Mom and Dad had created in the backyard in the middle of a green but otherwise pondless neighborhood, were accorded their full significance. Nature was a good topic for us, and after I took up residence here, during our weekly phone visits, which she always insisted be "on her nickel," I would give my mom the natural historical news from around here and she'd keep me apprised of the bird life at her place. I now realize that it was my mother who instilled in me what Rachel Carson called "the sense of wonder," teaching by example as she delighted in the living creatures that caught her attention.

Pondering my late mother, missing her terribly, brought my work to a standstill. Like a lot of life in the winter, I came to a halt. As anyone who has known such a loss learns—and who among us hasn't?—grief undermines concentration. Perhaps consciousness is pinioned by the absolutes of death and is in constant, impotent rebellion. One's aliveness is testified by the pain of loss, which feels so total that nonbeing, its antithesis, demands to be, but cannot be, comprehended. The self is stymied by the immensity of death.

It's not that death is a total stranger here; it's just that most of our meetings have been courtesy of smaller beings, furry or six-legged Yoricks whose corpses I could hold in my hand and study with philosophical and taxonomic detachment, doing natural history the old-fashioned way. Although in the universities biology has gone genetic-reductionist and nature study is extracurricular, there was a time when the study of organisms was all necrology. Knowledge was pursued by examining collections of dead specimens or dissecting them. Corpses are convenient in not bolting, but other than that they don't behave. In my autodidact nature study, I never pass up an opportunity to look closely at another creature, dead or alive.

Living lawnless in the country means the woods and weeds come right up to my doorstep. My negligent landscaping makes diverse wildlife habitats and many opportunities to witness pint-sized dramas of life and death. One afternoon, I chanced on the corpse of a vole that had died for no obvious reason. Voles are the single most common mammal in the bioregion. Such abundant life-forms are nature's all-you-can-eat buffet. Their rodent numerousness puts them on many a predator's menu, and their furtiveness means that they're not a free lunch. Maybe the cat had pounced on this vole and scared it to death, but there was no sign of injury on its velvet body. I held all two inches of it in my bare palm and examined it, looking closely at its pointy snout, its delicately articulated paws, and its barely discernable pinpoint eyes. "A mouse is miracle enough to stagger six billion infidels," wrote Walt Whitman, and so is a vole. Compounding the miracle was an amber flea that hopped from the dead vole onto my palm, living proof that there are worlds within worlds. Aware of the fact that some fleas themselves may host still tinier organisms, such as the bacterium *Yersinia pestis*, the cause of the plague, I placed the vole back on the ground, laying the great table with carrion. I dusted my hands, hoping that my zoological curiosity would not lead to epidemiological news and my cadaver becoming an object of someone else's study.

Here, life and death are closer by and various. Matt, one of my neighbors, is a successful taxidermist and farmer. He is a bright, energetic, and outgoing young husband and father. Matt does excellently whatever he turns his hand to, be it wildlife biology or farming. I stopped by his place one day before winter got under way to see whether he could sell me some fresh straw bales to gird the base of my writing studio. We wound up talking about cats. I have a house cat; they've got barn cats. Barn cats are working members of the homestead, and theirs is not an easy life. Matt said that barn cat life got a little softer at their place when his wife began to worm and feed them. With the barn cat meal program, however, came a resurgence of mice in the grain bin. In the hungry old days, said Matt, one of the cats would perch on his shoulder while he was feeding the cattle and scoot down his arm to pounce on any mice that were flushed when a hay bale was moved.

Barn cats might live three or four years, Matt guessed. A house cat, if lucky, can go for fifteen or more. Barn cats face a legion of perils. Coyotes relish kittens. They come down out of the hills behind Matt's farmstead, saunter past the malamute and husky in their chain-link pen, and help themselves to the kitten spread in the barn. It makes me sad to think of kittens killed by coyotes, and I wonder whether such losses sadden the queen who bore the litter. I don't wonder whether she pities the mouselings she orphans by her hunting. Having most of your offspring devoured from within by parasites or from without by predators is just the way it goes for most of the wild things, for death and birth in perfect balance keep the wheel of life in motion. In our synthetic environments, we've come to expect a ripe old age, even for our pets, as a right, and to regard any foreshortening as tragic. How keen was the experience of living when there was no such expectation? One would sing one's death song every day. It's the strong and watchful, wily kitten who lives to be a barn cat.

Simone, my house cat, had a brother, Tyrone, who was also dear to me, and although the body of cat literature is probably sufficient by now, I include the following sad cat story because it gave me a foretaste of a sorrowing to come.

Several years ago, as I set off in my car to give a talk down-state, I discovered Tyrone, a big, sweet tiger cat, dead, stiff, and gritty at the edge of the pavement a quarter mile from home. He'd been struck by some vehicle and, I can only hope, died instantly. Tyrone had been AWOL since the previous after-noon—a longish time for him to be away—and I'd begun to fear exactly this. It started raining as I picked him up. I gave him a hasty burial out back behind the house, digging a hole, cursing, and wailing. Simone watched, curious, from a little distance as I shoveled. I sprinkled catnip and salt tears in Tyrone's grave, tossed in his favorite plaything, and then laid his handsome body in the ground. It was some hard labor to shovel in the dirt to entomb and absorb this hearty pet, who had been a delight for the past seven years.

I stopped by the home of Tom, my gardening beau, for lunch and consolation before I resumed my trip. The great transformation just begun begged a question: "Where's Tyrone? Every material thing that he was is still here, and he's gone forever." "Every material thing that he was, was here before he existed," added Tom.

So what is it that's just passing through?

I've reached that certain age at which the ability to write a decent note of condolence, console a widow, or join in mourn-ing a parent's death gets too frequent exercise. Epicurus believed that death was final, that there was one life per cus-tomer, so it was wisdom to live it well. Since death was noth-ing, we must not be sad. "Sweet is the memory of a dead friend," he wrote. Yet however genuine his equanimity, the philosopher, too, grieved, saying, "Let us show our feeling for our lost friends not by lamentation but by meditation."

In the Epicurean view of nature, all that exists is atoms and void. The soul, then, has substance, of a delicate sort. Lucretius' poetic genius twined and flowered around the proposition of arguing the soul's consubstantiality with the body and thus its mortality:

> Soul must not be held exempt
> from being born or privileged not to die.
> We must not think that souls so closely knit
> to the body could ever have slipped in from outside;
> plain facts declare against this whole idea.
> For soul is so bound to viscera, sinew, vein,
> and bone, that even the teeth share in sensation:
> witness decay, the shock of ice-cold water,
> and the harsh crunch of a bite on grit in bread.
> The soul is part of the fabric; it can't leave
> undamaged, you see, or free itself intact.

Whether or not souls die is impossible to know, but Lucretius' sensational analogies also speak to the gut-wrenching quality of the pains that afflict the soul.

There's a lot of cancer around. The tumor in my mother's lung grew so slowly that the oncologist was a bit baffled. That slowness permitted our family three-quarters of a year to love Mama following her terminal diagnosis. Our family ran true to form, but with more gravity. The same day my mother informed me of her fatal illness, I learned that another feisty old woman, my great friend Ramona, had succumbed at last to her lung cancer. Ramona had gone about her dying in charac-ter, too, with sometimes discomforting candor. Over the previous few years, out in California, five men, former colleagues, highly gifted writers and editors and a designer, had all died in their early fifties of cancer. Nearer to home, another acquaintance was, as she mentioned almost in passing when we happened to speak, outliving her doctor-decreed lung cancer death sentence by a year and a half. Her composure about what she was facing was remarkable, and I said as much. It was hard, she said; the hardest part was not being able to assume a future, not being able to expect to get around to doing this, that, or the other thing *someday*.

Of course, all our days are as numbered as the hairs on our heads. Any healthy one of us could step out in traffic, slip in the bathtub, or be struck dead by a meteorite, leaving behind friends suffering from terminal cancer to attend our funerals. True enough, but most of us who can, live toward the morrow and do assume the future.

So far as I know, I have no life-threatening illness. Yet as I savor the presence of nature in this place, I fear not that I may not pass this way again but that this way itself is passing fast. The number of blazing pink surveyor's flags in the neighborhood—like the telltale lesions of Kaposi's sarcoma—do not augur well for such integrity of landscape as still remains. The property lines are being drawn, and quartered. Heavy equipment, deforestation, erosion, and pole barns are bound to follow.

"Growth for the sake of growth is the ideology of the cancer cell," said Edward Abbey. As without, so within. The ideology of growth is willing to sacrifice lives for what is advertised as progress, whether they're human sacrifices sanctioned by the calculus of acceptable risk or the lives of the myriad creatures destroyed in the name of development. These malignancies of sprawl and terminal illness ordain that nothing in this life, be it my sense of self or my immediate surroundings, will ever be the same again.

As I write this at more of a remove from my mother's death, the pain is resolving into tenderness. I can appreciate the change this loss wrought. I have standing now in the company of the bereaved, the knowledge of how it feels, and the sense of what might comfort another, even as I was comforted and helped to live on through the grief as time crawled painfully slow from fall into winter and then a new year.

That February blew warm, then cold. A freakish southwest wind dissipated the snow, exposed the weeds, and bared some earthy banks. The thaw concentrated the winter's accumulation of dust and crud sullying the snow's surface, making all things drear.

Around Valentine's Day, the cold came back with a vengeance. A front raced in, pushing a line of thunderstorms northeast across the region and towing a wave of bitter temperatures that froze the meltwater, the saturated ground, and the shrunken snows to ringing hardness. Finally, it blew in four or five inches of light, dry snow. The next day, the landscape was white again with fresh snow and the sun was shining.

That afternoon, there was the clear possibility of a ski and there were plenty of needful things to do, but my first move was to escape from my sadness into a nap on the couch, balled up warm and oblivious under a heavy comforter. When I awoke, the sunlight was still playing through the scattered clouds. There were still things needing to be done in the studio and in the house; however, I decided to accept the sweet magic maker's invitation to arise from the slough of despond and put on my skis. My one ironclad certainty—that it's always a good idea to go for a swim—has a winter corollary: Whenever possible, it's always a good idea to go for a ski. With its rhythmic engagement of all four limbs and involvement with H$_2$O (though in its solid form), cross-country skiing is akin to swimming.

The day had grown warmer during the sun's brief appearance. However cold that "warmer" was, the early evening was calm, with the dread windchill factor in abeyance. Out I went, trying to dodge the most menacing patches of gray, rippled ice, gliding mostly, scraping sometimes.

Sunset began to gild the treetops and tint the clouds. My sadness, that familiar dull ache in the gut, was with me, but it assumed a relative position among the efforts and sensations of movement, the piercing deliciousness of clean, cold breaths, and the intrigues of squirrel tracks and of mouse tunnels unroofed by the thaw. More color flooded the surroundings as the sun slipped lower, and I wanted to keep moving in this rosy radiance as long as I possibly could.

As I slid down the deep trail to the pond, I gained speed—too much. At the very second I was congratulating myself on my platonic relationship with gravity, I lost my balance and toppled backward into the snow. Awkwardly hauling myself back upright, I groaned out loud. Vertical once more, I skied the few dozen yards past the snow-bowed blackberry canes and bare-limbed poplar trees to the flat expanse of the pond, pink now with the last of the daylight.

Across the pond, on the north-facing bank where a grove of young hemlocks grows, I noticed a curlicue track moving out from under the trees and then onto the snowy, frozen flat surface. Where it stopped was a motionless hank of dark fur. I skied around the edge of the pond to investigate and came upon a porcupine curled on its side. The porky had waddled around under the tree and out on the snowy frozen surface of the pond and then collapsed. As I approached, it curled its body slightly and weakly flexed its forepaws. Its shining eye was open. Without much thinking, I picked it up and cradled it in my mittens, crooning dismay and sympathy.

Already I'd broken First Aid Rule Number One: Don't move the victim. The porcupine sighed and writhed. It was a beautiful creature, with lush ebony fur on its face and belly and no wounds visible. The spines on its back and tail were relaxed. The porky was too feeble to bristle. I carried it a few paces back to the hemlocks and laid it gently in a small warmth- and wind-sculpted hollow at the base of one of the trees. The porky stirred a little and sighed again. It sure looked to be dying.

I couldn't think of anything to do except doff my skis and sit with the porcupine on the snow, hoping I hadn't hurt it by carrying it back here. A half dozen of its spines had lodged in my right mitten. Moments passed. The porky cringed and sighed and didn't breathe its last. I couldn't manage just to sit there. Should I try to give it shelter? Cover it with branches? Build an igloo? Melt some snow and give it water? Wasn't there something I could do? Put it out of its misery? Haul it to the wildlife shelter? Recite the Porky Paramita Sutra?

This porcupine was a wild thing, it was dying, and it had no need of me. It could not feel my sympathy and may have suffered from my impulsive cradling. If it was still aware of my presence, it was probably sore afraid. Fancy this: Some big, strange animal comes upon you in your death throes, scoops you up, lays you down in the place you just set out from, and then sits near you and stares anxiously.

My sitting was melting the snow and chilling me to my foundation. Not only had I not brought along my vial of arnica for homeopathic first aid or any tobacco for a sacred offering, I had neither a ground cloth nor the yogic discipline to keep a vigil in the snow during the porcupine's last hours—no patience to await the final stillness, the dulling eyes. I got up and retraced the porcupine's erratic track, wandering the few feet from the base of two young crossed trees to the hemlock where it now lay. There were a couple of yellowish spots in the snow. Was that urine? What had brought the porcupine to this extremity? Disease? Starvation? A fall? Thirst? Poison?

However it comes, we've all got to die. My mother got to die, I get to die, and the porky accomplished its dying during the nightlong hours after we met. Death is one of the great shaping powers on this planet and in the human mind. My mother's death and the deaths of friends have tinctured my consciousness. Although a couple of years have passed since Mama died, I'm only now assuming the fact of her silence. Even so, I miss her, especially her voice, every day. There's no way not to have a heavy heart for a long while after one's mother has died. This heart grew in her.

There's no way out but through, taking one step after another, doing the next necessary thing. Mourning is like picking your way across a torrent, rock by rock, with the likelihood of a slip and a soaking, and the knowledge that there's a lot of stumbling yet to do, undercutting your will. You fall down and then gather your wits. You stand up and step forth, bruised but without a better idea of what to do, and then you continue as the sun swings lower in the sky and the nights lengthen.

Whatever its magnitude, the loss must be faced. Respite in the company of a friend is a blessing, but the reality of loss does not abate. The wood in the stove burns away; the ashes must be carried out and more wood carried in. What a mercy is the obviousness of dirty dishes, dusty floors, and dwindling firewood. It is a relief, a comforting simplicity of action, to tend to the daily necessities.

The call of life is strong in me, strong enough finally to trump grief and depression. Long live the living. That's how life persists—in the bodies of the living and through the living of it. May all beings—mice and voles, chickadees and squirrels, grasses and streams, pines and poplars, fleas and coyotes, parents and offspring, blackberries and hemlocks, cats and porcupines—persist! And may I, too, persist a while in living this life my parents gave to me.

10

OUR COMMON FATE

Epicurean simplicity suggests that we learn to recognize the pain excess causes and learn to recognize and enjoy a decent sufficiency. Lucretius saw the futility of coursing after every want:

> For what's on hand, if we've learned nothing sweeter
> so far, we like the best and deem superb;
> then, often, some later and better discovery
> destroys the old and alters our
> feeling toward it. . . .
>
> For us, what harm to lack
> our gold, our purples stiff with rich brocade,
> while we have plain, coarse cloth to keep us warm?
> Yes, all for nothing we wretched men toil on
> forever, and waste our lives on foolishness;
> clearly, because we never learned the limits
> of having, and where true pleasure's growth must end.

Several years ago, at a teach-in in Berkeley, California, organized by the International Forum on Globalization, I heard a speech by Wolfgang Sachs, a German scholar and author who is among the most astute critics of conventional development strategies. In the course of his remarks, he spoke of the "subterranean relationship between pleasure and austerity." This phrase struck me as having real charm, as in magic. Sachs, project director of the Wuppertal Institute for Climate, Environment and Energy, spoke also of the institute's work to promote design solutions that could reduce Germany's consumption of materials and energy by 80 to 90 percent. "Limits are the new frontiers," he said. Versed in sociology, theology, and history, Sachs bejeweled his compact and original speech with proverbs for our time and uttered many a charm against waste and anomie.

In austerity, true pleasure becomes clear. In profligate times, austerity is where beauty waits. Austerity is at one with the grace necessity sculpts. Austerity entails both self-restraint and the capacity for abandonment—in a task, in friendship and contemplation, or in the phenomenal. There is no poverty or meagerness, but volition, in austerity. One can savor every least thing—the faint tang of skunk lingering under the bird feeder, the warm scratch of wool blankets, the jade tree in the dry cleaner's window, the flavor of bread, the accents and rhythms of the talk on the bus. Wonder is a congenial discipline.

Although my aim in this book is to advocate material simplicity more by attraction than by exhortation, through sharing the mingled pleasures of this kind of living, I'd be remiss in not saying that in and of itself, simple living won't solve the dreadful problems besetting the biosphere. There's something dangerously oxymoronic when simple living becomes a theme of slick magazines. Simplicity needs to affect more than the household's discretionary budget. Billionaires living simply but failing to "divest and share"—another Oren Lyons dictum—won't suffice.

The disparity in incomes around the world continues to widen. Voluntary simplicity mocks the poor while holding the libertarian potential to divert attention from structural injustice. The simplicity craze will be worse than useless—merely a sectarian morality or personal aesthetic—if it leaves the corporate rascals and wealthy elite free to pursue a global climax of greed.

"If the lad or lass is among us who knows where the secret heart of this growth monster is hidden," wrote Gary Snyder, "let them please tell us where to shoot the arrow that will slow it down."

Simplicity and freedom are much allied. The pleasure freely derived from food and water, from companionship and countryside or city life, from good work and lives well lived, has been severed, privatized, tarted up, and sold back to us through mass media whose policy is to reinforce the status quo, whose business is to advertise affluence, and whose vocabulary consists of vulgar sensationalism and cheap sentiment. Now we are slaves to the cash economy and buy our enjoyment.

Some reasonable people see benefits resulting from and therefore justifying the global enterprise that sponsors and profits from the commodification and packaging of all the pieces of everyday life, and there are fatalists who regard the increasing subversion of natural processes and organic experience by technology as an inevitable consequence of human nature, an ultimate triumph of the human over nature.

For every person who's pessimistic about the outcomes of the degradation of land and water, there are dozens who feel bound, for intellectual, strategic, or religious reasons, to argue that the trade-offs have been worth it; or they say, "It's not necessarily dire," and argue that there could be other, less alarming constructions to make of the data. In any case, it's futile to try to promote public action by projecting scenarios of ecological doom, and it's heartless to limit the hopes of the up-and-coming generation. All those rejoinders have their elements of wisdom.

Unfortunately, such well-intentioned arguments are useful to transnational corporations and their client governments, whose public relations efforts employ scientists and economists to say that what one is seeing is not really ugliness but progress and that one's friend's lymphoma was an individual instance, not part of the cancer epidemic caused by the radioactive and toxic by-products of industry. Land speculators and construction interests plead that it's unjust to lock out the increasing numbers of everybodies who only want the same chance to subdivide and occupy the land that everybody who preceded them had. A babel of denial, good intentions, bad intentions, propaganda, and apparent reasonableness impedes our society from confronting the severe reality of the planet's degradation and making a commensurate response.

Some friends, capable of more limberness of imagination and metaphysical credulity than I'll ever muster, trust that the universe knows what it's doing. After all, there have been other mass extinctions, so there must be an evolutionary reason for this one. What bothers me is that this time, our species is playing the part of the asteroid that hits the earth and wipes out the majority of its evolutionary lineages. This is difficult to square with the idea that *Homo sapiens* is the crown of cognition, leading edge of conscious evolution, organ of the planet's self-perception. Was this our only possible destiny?

Cultural historian Thomas Berry speaks of the possible inception of an "Ecozoic era." Our species has concluded the Cenozoic era, the period that brought forth the mammals, birds, and flowering plants. In the Ecozoic, it will be our job to restore and foster evolutionary relationships among whatever life-forms happen to survive. The ecological optimum—a low human population and high biodiversity—is long gone. We are left to establish the Ecozoic among what the distinguished zoologist Raymond Dasmann called "the tattered remnants of the old, wild world."

Although I don't frequent the wilderness, I believe my deep-ecologist friends who trek into the dwindling expanses of roadless land and, in a relation to the wild unmediated by technology other than boots, tent, stove, and backpack, innocent of any intention to remake it, say that only there do they discover what it means to be fully human. Given that the greater part of our history as human beings was spent in direct relation with untamed land, it makes sense that the full realization of human nature would be found through austerity in the larger community of the wild.

The romance of the primitive has it that once upon a time before civilization, human experience was full and seamless, embedded in nature, governed by ecological necessity. Human life was fraught with pleasure, pain, plenty, or privation, depending on the abundance of game, the use of fire, and the coming of rain or of ice, and always on paying attention. Uncivilized humankind, in its roaming little bands, did less work and more schmoozing, had a better diet, got more sleep, and didn't have a long life expectancy. Even after the agricultural revolution, shortness of average life span—a twenty-five-year life expectancy at birth—continued to be the common lot in Europe until the changes wrought during the industrial era.

In September 1997, I spent my second night as a forty-nine-year-old lying, if not doing much sleeping, on the hard, damp ground in a kind of fairy circle hidden in a little fir plantation out back on my property. My field trip helped me understand why, among our hunter-gatherer ancestors, even with their organic diets, daily exercise, and earth-centered spirituality, thirty years was a lot of longevity to hope for. After a few decades of sleeping on the ground wrapped in a pelt, Grandma would wake up feeling crippled on most mornings and might not be able to keep up with the rest of the band in its continuous foraging.

In my cohort of fifty-somethings, we observe our parents, who are in their seventies and eighties, "slowing down." Slowing down can work in a suburb or a retirement home, but you can't get away with it very long in the outback. In the Paleolithic good old days, the band one day, with great regret, would have to put together a little bit of food and water and make a somewhat safe and comfortable place to leave sloweddown Grandma, who would take that as her cue to die of natural causes, like wolves or jackals.

I went out to my backyard temple ground and got what felt like terminal lumbago in order to hear the night sounds better, for one thing—coyotes had been quite tuneful right about then—and to prove to myself that I still had the old moxie. In these Milquetoast adventures, I usually learn that I do have the moxie and that it's getting older. I'd had a pretty good day in and out of my writing studio, but by nightfall I was bored and restless. I was fresh out of good, clean trash and didn't have the high resolve to begin reading an actual literary work. The night promised to be clear and not cold, so I decided on the spur of the moment to divert myself by camping out.

I fetched my seldom-seen sleeping bag and pad from a dark, crowded closet shelf. (Notice that the greenhorn didn't take a ground cloth.) I assembled the gear for a small ritual: a candle and matches, tobacco, sage, sweet grass, and cedar incense. I also gathered up a flashlight, notebook, and pencil;

citronella insect repellent; and drinking water. In the last of the dusk, in the light of the moonrise, I made my way through the gathering dark the half mile to the fir stand with Simone, my faithful feline companion. I moved carefully, bearing in mind that however safe this expedition, twisting an ankle was still a possibility. As I made my way, I realized that over the past decade-plus, I had come to know this terrain pretty well, enough that moving through the waist-high bracken ferns of late summer no longer spooked me. Since this country is bereft of big wild animals, the only conceivable danger to me would be from my own carelessness or my own kind—some poacher sneaking into the center of the section on the ad hoc road, a two-track (so called because in this sandy land, if you drive your big, old truck off the beaten path, others will follow the two tracks of its tires and a road will happen).

My destination, a hidden clearing near the south property line, had been accumulating mana for years through spring-time lovemaking, visits from special friends, solitary visits, and offerings. When I came back from India with jugs of water from the Ganges River to decant into little brass bottles and give to a handful of friends, I sprinkled the remainder in the fairy circle there. I would be sleeping under the stars in a spot that had been severally consecrated and must be on my best behavior.

On arrival, I put down my gear, and then in an approximate way I cast a circle of invocation and protection. I lit the candle, made an offering of a pinch of tobacco, and with incenses hailed the spirits of the four directions. That done, I crawled into my sleeping bag, not anticipating much sleep but hoping for the company of Others. At moonset, there was a quick cantata of eldritch yodels somewhere to the southwest. Also, in the colonnades of big red pines to the northwest, some harsh barks. A fox?

Most of the night sounds issued from truck traffic on the state highway half a mile south, with the occasional raucous buzz of a motorcycle to vary monotony. There was also a periodic "Crump!" that I thought might be made by a percussion device to frighten away scavengers from the landfill south of the highway. I listened, and thought about the birds and rodents and deer and raccoons, all the animals whose lives depend on the acuity of their senses, especially hearing. What was all that road din doing to their ears, pricked in the dark and sensitive enough to detect the approach of footpads and a pounce, but blasted instead with high-decibel gear changes and tires whining on asphalt?

As the hours passed, I lay there snugged up in my bag, feeling (mistakenly, as it proved) pretty comfortable for sleeping out on the ground. There were a couple of shooting stars for wishing. Living on the outskirts of the galaxy and gazing up at the constellations and the Milky Way couldn't persuade me of my insignificance. The Pleiades, Cepheus and Cassiopeia, Perseus, Pegasus, Andromeda, Cygnus, and Draco (according to the star map I consulted later) were all twinkling overhead as I tossed and turned in the sleeping bag. Every so often, the cat would stop by the drawstring aperture at the top of the bag, which was cinched up so that only my nose was exposed to the open air. Simone would sniff and give a little purr and then resume her position a few feet away. So the night went.

The plan was to emulate my hero Aldo Leopold and awaken to the first light of dawn and its birdsong, to lie there under the open sky listening to each new voice joining the chorus. Actually, Leopold would have been up and dressed well before dawn and have a pot of coffee going on the fire. He'd have had his notebook open and his pencil poised to record each singer in its turn. He'd have known the birds by their songs as well as by their appearance. Fatigued by hours of shifting around in search of a tolerable position, after I finally got to sleep, I didn't awake till broad daylight. By then, the only sounds to be heard were trucks again, and crickets.

I gathered up my gear, remembered my etiquette and thanked the four directions before departing the circle, and headed for my writing studio to get some supplemental sleep on the napping couch there. Five hours later, I awoke stiff as a board with lumbago and scarcely able to walk. In order to get myself some breakfast, I had to move. If I hadn't needed to buffer the aspirin I meant to gobble, I might have opted for a fast as being more comfortably stationary.

Someday, an ability to sleep on the ground could prove useful. There may not always be a bed to sleep upon. Many millions of people are sleeping tonight on packed earth floors without benefit of mattresses. How do those women feel when they wake up before dawn and have to walk ten miles to fetch the family's firewood or drinking water?

Given the critical condition of the biosphere, I fear that all too often I feel justified in being shrill. Enough bad news and that chord of apocalypse latent in the sense of history in a Christian ambit twangs deafeningly. The puritan strain in the ecology movement is hardly surprising. What spurs such puritanism is different from a doctrinal dispute; the ecological crisis has objective reality. Epicurean though I would be, holy pleasure is not my life's only guide. Guilt, too, leads me around by the nose. My guilt usually devolves from the thought of what my choices are doing to the Others. I observe a goodly number of personal taboos to dodge that guilt.

Taboos have long been quite effective means of shaping lifeways, but, like magic, they're more likely to work if they flow with some vital tendency. In most cultures' earlier times, the wise folk took it upon themselves to evaluate individual and household preferences in terms of their effects on the commonweal. The preferences that threatened to undermine the culture would be interdicted and divine authority invoked to enforce these taboos. Taboos have to begin with a kernel of practical value—for group harmony, wildlife management, food safety, or eugenics. After a while, a patina of tradition tones down the glare of a "because God said so" rationale. Hence, the late-breaking, arbitrary, state-sponsored taboo "Just say no to drugs" is tremendously ineffectual despite the militarized enforcement. Even animals seek out the plant medicines that will get them high. Yet certain once-useful taboos still have their authority: Moslems and Jews abstain from pork (pigs didn't do well in Middle Eastern climates). Equally venerable proscriptions still serve well: Hindus don't kill cows (it's foolish to slay one's tractor and primary source of curds). Could the practices and pleasures of simplicity develop into sensible taboos to restrain human actions that degrade the biosphere, unarguably the basis of the commonweal?

After a swim one summer day at the nearby lake, as I mounted my bicycle I asked a little boy who was seining for minnows if he would put them back, thinking that he might just be catching them to get a closer look. "No," he replied brightly, "We use them for fishing bait." I said nothing but pedaled off, fantasizing some uninvited taboo-tossing peda-gogy, starting with "Only take as many as you need. If there aren't enough little fish left in the lake to grow up, then in a year or so there won't be any big fish to catch and eat." Then a pathetic fallacy: "Try to imagine that those little fish—the fishes' kids—have feelings just like yours." Further research, however, disclosed that minnows aren't juvenile but are small grown-ups. Even if, despite being a deep-ecological spinster, I am nonetheless a member of the village that it takes to raise a child, it was just as well that I spared that child my misinformed sermonette. Besides, fishers can be natural historians and waterside contemplatives par excellence.

My salvific vision is that if everyone could experience some joyous, muscle-powered liberty of the body and fascinating fraternity with nature, then faster, noisier, fossil-fueled modes of engaging the world would fall away. This is perilously close to saying, "What a grand world it would be if everyone could just be like me"—not the everyday real me, of course, but the idealized me-projection. The moment I needed something practical, like the services of a good mechanic or a week's groceries, and came to find out that everyone who had hitherto been doing their jobs within the getting and spending paradigm had seen the light and wandered off to muse on the butterflies and the minnows, the flaw in my nature-epiphany fantasy would materialize.

As I bicycled home through the short, dim tunnel of broad-leaved trees that shades the dirt road, one red-spotted purple butterfly caught my eye, fanning its wings as it rested on the damp, packed earth. Then another butterfly, dancing in the brighter space where the lake road meets the pavement, delighted me, too. I felt more affiliation with these insects, and with whatever warbler was singing up in the green canopy, felt happier to be in their company, than I ever feel about sharing the lakeside with a gaggle of humanity—local moms, dads, and little boys seining minnows, all of us refreshing ourselves in our various ways at the water's edge.

The reader may have noted a tinge of misanthropy to this epicurean. Unless those humans happen to be field biologists, modern novelists, or organic farmers, it's creatures other than her fellow humans that enjoy her highest regard. In my pagan philosophy, nature is not the problem; culture is the problem.

A culture that would understand and disavow humanity's imperialism in nature could be quite an improvement for all concerned.

Just as Epicurus could not conceive of a good that excluded the pleasures afforded by the senses, I can't conceive of a good that does not include some engagement with wild beings in free nature. Wonder is our erotic affiliation with all of life. If we develop this, enjoy it, and follow its promptings, our wants will be fewer and our needs plainer. "Those who contemplate the beauty of earth," said Rachel Carson, "will find reserves of strength that will endure as long as life lasts."

For human beings to "live unknown," or no more known than the thrashers and monarchs and hylae, might be a workable search image. The creativity of Malcolm Wells, whose underground architecture envisions handsome, contemporary settlements designed so that the soil isn't buried under our shelters but shelters us and can still host green life, comes to mind, as does John Todd's invention of solar-powered water purification systems that bring together novel but native aquatic ecosystems—the "Living Machines" of Ocean Arks International—to treat municipal sewage or to restore degraded water bodies biologically rather than chemically. These individuals and hundreds of other ecological designers and "bioneers" are sensitive apprentices to the magic maker and don't seek to be Faustian magi.

Because they are tangles of interacting forces, all the scenarios are shifting fast. Climate change ramifies throughout systems; so does the introduction of exotic species and of hormone-disrupting chemicals. Biologists speak of "cascades" of extinctions, for no species is an island. Even running over a squirrel in Anytown, U.S.A., means there's one less tree planter at work. Now that these big, systemic derangements are becoming more evident, I discover that I, too, have been in denial; I hadn't anticipated immersion in the big system-crashing consequences, not here, not yet. But in the summer of 1999, for the first time, there were wads of algae rocking under Lake Michigan's waves on the rippled, sandy bottom of Whaleback Bay.

Lake Michigan is oligotrophic—big, young, and cold, without much aquatic plant life. Ordinarily, there's no conspicuous lake weed. By the mid-twentieth century, the lake's ecosystem had been revolutionized by the invasion of parasitic sea lampreys, which led to the virtual demise of the lake trout, thus eliminating the predator that might have kept the eruptions of another oceanic invader, a little fish called the alewife, in check. Now alewives, ill-adapted to freshwater life, proliferate wildly in the lake but die en masse, littering the beaches by the decomposing millions.

That beach at Whaleback Bay was one of the stops on the whirlwind tour of the splendors of the county Phil conducted in honor of my initial visit in the summer of 1984. How novel to me and lovely it was to drive to a beach through a hardwood forest. There were groves of white cedars along the creek that flows into the bay, as well as oaks, maples, birches, and beeches. Thick by the edge of the dirt road were wild roses, grapes, and alders. Willow thickets made a portal to the foredunes, with their blowing fringes of beach grass. All this opened out to miles of pale, sandy beach and clear water. Coming from California, from the Pacific Rim, I hadn't realized that Lake Michigan is a freshwater sea. I certainly couldn't believe that such a beautiful beach could exist and not be completely aswarm with beachgoers.

It became my birthday custom to visit Whaleback Bay for a ceremonial swim. In mid-September 1995, it was a loner's day at the beach. There were only two other people in the whole expanse—a brilliant blue sky, turquoise waters deepening to ultramarine, a clean beach, the constant sound of waves, sunlight and warmth, and high, fine moiré clouds. I walked a long way south on the beach for the sheer, dumb pleasure of feeling myself walk.

Eventually, I stopped walking and went for a swim. The water was cold, but not heart-stopping. As I swam, I savored the lake's transparency and the clean, tawny color of the sandy bottom, looked through the water, seeing shapes, and looked landward to the long, sweeping curve of the beach, the pale, windswept whips of beach grass, the brooding, raw silhouettes of the white pines, and the lush hardwood foliage on the headlands.

By the 1980s, Lake Michigan's waters had received enough pesticides, including atrazine gone airborne and carried north from farmlands in the Mississippi River valley, and enough chlorinated hydrocarbons, polychlorinated biphenyls (PCBs), dioxin, and other hormone-mimicking compounds, to cause fish-eating waterfowl such as cormorants and gulls to produce deformed offspring or exhibit hermaphrodism. Fish-eating humans were being advised to limit their intake of Great Lakes fish.

The lake I met for the first time in 1984 was far from pristine, but for years after that, having swum in Lake Michigan, I could catch a whiff of the mineral freshness of clear water rather than of rotten alewives in my wet hair. This recent algae bloom was attributable to the siphoning activity of billions of zebra mussels. These invasive exotic mollusks had arrived in the Great Lakes via some oceangoing freighter's Baltic bilge water only in 1987. The zebra mussel plague cleans the water too much, reducing the lake's turbidity so dramatically that more sunlight penetrates, fostering certain kinds of algal growth.

The degradation of this inland sea has progressed from alewife infestation to bioaccumulation of toxic chemicals to pond slime in only a few years. Those clouds of algae in Whaleback Bay made blatant that there's no place to run, no place to hide, no "away" to get to. There's no natural feature too large to ruin.

Privately, quite a few of my fellow ecocentrics believe that the fight for the wild, for the health of the biosphere, is lost. The degradation of the land, oceans, and atmosphere is so widespread and acute that its momentum, they say, is unstoppable. What is interesting is the fact that we mostly believe that it behooves us to belie our gut sense of futility when we aren't talking only among ourselves. None of us plans to give up trying to accomplish our valiant ecological aims, to stop the extinction cascades, to save the wild, and to restore and reinhabit our life places. If we can get past the staggering practical, moral, and aesthetic implications of extinction's finality, then perhaps we can get on with the business of doing something Ecozoic with what remains. But the weeping is unavoidable.

In *The Heat Is On*, his book about global warming, Ross Gelbspan relates the following story:

> In January 1995, a vast section of ice the size of Rhode Island broke off the Larsen ice shelf in Antarctica.
>
> Dr. Rodolfo Del Valle, an Argentine scientist who witnessed the disintegration of the ice shelves [while] flying 6000 feet overhead in a light plane . . . saw that the ice shelf, up to 1000 feet thick in places, was beginning to break up into smaller icebergs. . . . [Del Valle said,] "The first thing I did was cry."

The paradox is that even though I cannot realistically foresee a future that doesn't appal me, the present still abounds in simple pleasures. However dismal the outlook, how could one fail to enjoy such once-ordinary, now-scarce phenomena as sweet, crisp air, soaking summer rains, and fireflies blinking in the swamp? For the past 4 billion years, this planet has been churning out the wonders: bacteria, nucleated cells, diatoms, jellyfish, slime molds, ruby-throated hummingbirds, goldfish, tiger moths, shield-shaped beetles sporting the colors of an okra blossom, tamaracks, sturgeons, and thirteen-lined ground squirrels. Natural phenomena, with their implicate beauty, their grandeur, and their proportion, could, by any measure meaningful to us ephemera, be regarded as infinite.

Some of this sense of nature's infinitude lies within the beholder. Ronald Reagan infamously declared that if you'd seen one redwood, you'd seen them all. Visionary urbanite William Blake, on the other hand, suggested: "To see a world in a grain of sand / And a heaven in a wild flower, / Hold infinity in the palm of your hand / And eternity in an hour."

Although there is an ethical imperative for humanity to desist from any further destruction of nature, my concern for earth's ecology is epicurean also, motivated by a pleasure that is not so small and slender. Some days, that curiosity about life as it manifests in the five kingdoms of biology is the Eros keeping me alive.

Thanatos and Eros have some relevance here: The death wish of civilization, its all-too-successful antipathy to wild nature, is producing circumstances—ecological breakdown—that would seem to justify a personal wish not to live on into a prosthetic future in which nature is weedy, domesticated, manipulated, and monotonous and artifacts dominate existence. There's an awful tension between the desire to witness and understand as much as I can of what philosopher David Abram felicitously terms "more-than-human nature" and the horror of the daily earth rape perpetrated by bulldozers, chain saws, pesticides, and all the vast armament of progress.

Despair is not a particularly respectable condition, yet despair and delight alternate like systole and diastole in my heart. Throughout my life, there have been moments when depression or despair have laid me so low that I've contemplated taking my own life, as my neighbor finally did. I've been helped to decide to continue living by friends, therapists, fellowship, and pharmacy. Were it not for my existential alliance with the larger life, none of this help would have availed.

Sometimes in the murk of a dark night of the soul, when I am desperate for a glimmer of a reason for being, I catechize myself: What if you could never hear another crow or never again feel the moss soft under your feet? What if you could never watch another caterpillar? What if you were never to see another snowfall or eat another apple? Would you want an end to those experiences?

One July morning a few years ago, I got out of bed and took a mug of tea onto the back deck to sit and sip in the full sun. I watched a scruffy, voluble chickadee busy itself in one of the cherry trees. A female hummingbird visited the feeder, making a big noise coming and going. On the beat-up locust shrub that has volunteered right next to the porch, I noticed half a dozen different kinds of insects, among them a lovely little black wasp with a dash of vermilion on her abdomen, some coral-colored aphid-like critters, and a lime green katydid-like animal casting a sharp, linear shadow. As ever, I felt a sense of community with all these remarkable beings. Their insides are real. They are individuals with real lives and important business in this world. Some of them pair off. A lot of them look after their young. Surely they, too, feel a sense of release when the sun returns to warm things up and dry things out after a few days of slashing rainstorms.

I took off my nightshirt and sat there palely naked as the next animal. With the sunlight on my skin and the good air to enfold us, I felt that I was in the body of my Mother, very much a part of the earth's living tissue.

There is a sense in which it matters not what may come. A life alert to simple pleasures, with perception cultivated and attuned to beauty, and a large capacity for friendship can serve us well come what may, be it Ecotopia, corporate fascism, or Armageddon. Whatever befalls, it behooves us to honor the moment by savoring what there is: light and shadow, bitter and sweet, harsh and tender, fragrant and foul, lyric and discord.

If we cultivate our delight in and gratitude for the least thing—a drink of water, a night's rest, the sight of a blue jay— we cultivate the life strong within us and enliven possibility itself. Although I fancy being a nun in a contemplative order with a membership of one, I sense that learning the limits of having, remembering the nature of true pleasure, and becoming the change I wish in the world involve finding a way to talk with that kid catching minnows, and, more important, to listen to him.

Acknowledgments

Epicurean Simplicity began with a suggestion from Deanne Urmy, at that time senior editor at Beacon Press, with whom I'd had the pleasure and privilege of working on my book *In Service of the Wild*. Deanne, a darn fine bookwoman, encouraged and supported the idea of the book and wished it well when it found its home at Island Press.

Katinka Matson, a leonine goddess guised as a literary agent, coached me through rewrites of the proposal and a dark night of the ego, then heartened me to "have an explosion"—write my own book for its own sake.

Legions of writers revere Barbara Dean, sage, nurturing, masterful executive editor at Island Press. Throughout our three-books-long working relationship she's been all of that and become a cherished friend.

When, upon first meeting Jonathan Cobb, executive editor of Island's Shearwater Books, I confessed to a writer's block, Jonathan intervened with warmth, wit, and seasoned intelligence: another friendship founded.

With a lot of help from Barbara, Jonathan, and others, the block was busted. Dottie Webb, Gilda Povolo, Anne-Marie Oomen, Bronwyn Jones, Rabbi Stacie Fine, Amy Elena Cook, and Loraine Anderson, members of the Child-free Women's Mindworkers Union Local #1, our writers' group, were chief among those helpers, the best of *compañeras* and labor coaches. Dottie, Gilda, Bronwyn, and Loraine read the second draft of the book and commented helpfully, as did my Berkeleyite friend Charlotte Robertson, with her fine eye and consummate literary taste. Collaborating with Glenn Wolff, the multitalented Boardman City dweller whose graphic artistry adds grace notes to this volume, has fulfilled a longstanding wish to see his images and my words gigging together on the page. Pat Harris's copyediting was sensitive, improving, and illuminating. Every writer should be so fortunate!

Julia Cameron's invaluable book *The Artist's Way* provided excellent counsel and, when I followed it, a happier way of working. *The Artist's Way* catalyzed another sustaining women's group. Mary Sharry, Laurie Leiser, Anita Fatjo (the artist formerly known as Cathy Look), Elizabeth Buzzelli, Melissa Burns, and I met weekly, trod the Way, ate pie, spoke from our hearts about our lives and our art, and helped one another to get on with the work.

Staff therapists for *Epicurean Simplicity* were the shrewd and kind Lois Martindale, Ph.D., whom I seem to have driven into retirement, and Lyn Conlon, M.D., a great shrink and true physician. For their skills and compassion I am deeply grateful.

A bequest from Ramona Morgan allowed me to undertake this book. Formidable and loving, Ramona left a vacancy in scores of lives when she died.

Gifts from Hunter and Hildegarde Hannum have supported this and previous works. The greatest gift, though, is our precious friendship.

Good ol' Dad champions my work and has more than once bailed out his impecunious daughter. Bless him.

Finally, there's Mama. No life, writing or otherwise, for S. Mills without her sacrifice, care, and devotion. She's gone now, but Dad says she would have been proud of me for this one. I hope that's right, and that *Epicurean Simplicity* attests all that my mother gave me and betokens the extraordinary woman that she was.

Index

Abbey, Edward, 183
Abram, David, 204
Abstinence, 198
Acid rain, 150
Activism, 29
Ahimsa (nonviolence), 72
Altar, 37–39. *See also* Ritual
Alvord, Katie, *Divorce Your Car!*, 98, 101
American heartland. *See* Midwest (upper)
Angwúsnasomtaqa (Hopi kachina), 37–38
Animism, 42
Anti-intellectualism, 140–41
Antler doll, 39
Aridgjis, Homero, 80–83, 84–85
Arts: the artist's life, 132; lack of public support for, 140–41. *See also* Writing
Austen, Jane, 144–45
Autobiographical narratives and persons, 9; automobile accident, 9, 118, 176–77; childhood and family, 6–7, 109–11, 125, 128, 147–48; coop board service, 119–20, 121–22; death of the author's mother, 16, 177, 178–79,

182–84, 187; graveyard visit, 99–100; the house, 9–10, 30–32; living in the Bay Area, 7–8, 114–15, 116; move to the upper Midwest, 8–10, 11–12; neighbor's suicide, 104–5; Phil, 8–9, 51, 118, 176; Rob, 10, 19; swimming, 88–90, 92–93; Tom, 52–53; trips (*See also* Sierra Chinqua), 57, 129
Automobile accident (autobiographical), 9, 118, 176–77
Automobiles, 98, 101
Autumn, 147, 149–50, 151, 152–53

Barn cats, 180–82
Beck, Simone, Louisette Bertholle, and Julia Child, *Mastering the Art of French Cooking*, 111
Beech tree, 150, 166; beech bark disease, 160
Beetle, Asian longhorn, 150
Benares (trip to), 129
Bereavement process, 16–17, 187–88. *See also* Death
Berg, Peter, 44
Berkeley Co-op, 115, 116

Bernie the storekeeper (author's friend), 36–37
Berry, Thomas, 192–93
Bicycles and cycling, 96–100, 102–5
Biodiversity, 168
Birds, 43–44, 205; backyard habitats, 63–64; corvid family, 42–43; juncos, 43; magpies, 44, 46; mockingbird, 44; phoebes, 45; robins, 44; thrashers, 44–48
Boardman City, 4, 115; food cooperative, 117–22
Boletes, 151–52
Books and literature, 141–45
Borrowing, 59–60
"bread labor," 138
British Museum, 144
Brower, David, *Let the Mountains Talk, Let the Rivers Flow*, 76
Brower, Lincoln, 84
Bush, George Sr., 159
Butterflies and caterpillars (*Lepidoptera*): metamorphosis of, 77–79; monarch butterflies, 76, 77–79; monarch caterpillars, 76, 78, 80; viceroy butterflies, 80. *See also* Monarch butterfly reserves

Cancer, 182–84
Carson, Rachel, 73, 178, 200
Cats: barn cats, 180–82; housecats, 181
Cheney, Simeon Pease, 46
Childhood and family, 6–7, 109–11, 125, 128, 147–48
Child, Julia, 111–12
Childlessness by choice, 12
Chinatown, 114
Chinese cuisine, 113–14

Class, income disparity, 131, 191
Clear-cutting, 166
Climate change, global, 28, 88, 159–61, 173–74, 200, 203
Coal production, 158
CoEvolution Quarterly, 34
Coldness, 170–71. *See also* Winter
Communication, 136; face-to-face, 120; letter writing, 136–37
Community, 122
Computers, 134, 135–36, 137–38
Consumer electronics, 33, 36; computers, 134, 135–36, 137–38; planned obsolescence and, 138; television, 32–33
Consumerism, 3, 4, 6–7, 82; environmental pollution and, 28
Convenience, 37
Conviviality, 107
Cooke, Mervyn, *Jazz*, 48
Cooking, 108–9, 177; dinner parties, 111, 112–13; family cooking, 109–11; gourmet meals, 114–15
Coop board service (autobiographical), 119–20, 121–22
Corporations, 136
Counterculture, 169
Coyotes, 180
Crop domestication, 55
Cross-country skiing, 176–77, 184–85
Crow Mother kachina doll, 37–38, 39
Cycles of nature, 90–91
Cycling and bicycles, 96–100, 102–5

Dasmann, Raymond, 193

Dass, Ram, 22
Davis, Adelle, *Let's Cook It Right*, 115
Death: and the art of life, 23–24; of the author's mother, 16, 177, 178–79, 182–84, 187; death cart effigy, 39; as the end (Epicurus), 23, 181; graveyard visit, 99–100; the mourning process, 16–17, 187–88
Deep ecology, 30, 192–93
Deer hunting, 153
"Depression spaghetti," 110
Despair, 205
Details and small things, 2, 11, 29
Development, 91–92; suburban sprawl, 92, 148
Divorce (autobiographical), 9, 51
Domesticated plants and animals, 55
Donne, John, 122
Dragonflies, 93–94
Durning, Alan Thein, *How Much Is Enough?*, 6

Earth Mother/Mother Nature, 162, 206
Ecology, 131; deep ecology, 30, 192–93
Ecology center, 169
Economic self-reliance, 115–16
Ecozoic era, 192–93
Ejido (communal landholding), 82
Elliot, Lang, *The Calls of Frogs and Toads*, 67
Entertaining, 111, 112–13
Environmental degradation, 95, 150, 167–68, 191–92, 197, 200–201; and consumerism, 28; and the future, 203–6; greenhouse effect, 28, 88,

159–61, 173–74, 200, 203; of inland lakes, 202–3; pollution, 72–73
Epicureanism: death as the end, 23, 181; on friendship, 123; the physical universe in, 24–25, 182; quietism and, 26–27; refinement of taste, 21; simplicity in, 2, 19, 189–90; the soul, 182. *See also* Simplicity
Epicurus, 2, 20–21, 23, 123, 200; garden of, 26–27, 113
Eros and Thanatos, 204
Everyday living, 24, 136. *See also* Simplicity
Exotic species, introduction of, 150, 200

Farming: factory farming, 50; organic farming, 107–8, 120. *See also* Gardening
Fax machine, 36
Feminine force, 161–62
Fire prevention, 163–64; by tree-cutting, 164–66
Firestorm, 163. *See also* Wildfire
Firewood, 157–58
Food coops, 115, 116–22; management issues, 119–20, 121–22
Forestry, industrial, 166
Forests: first-growth forests, 167; forest ecology, 167–68; hardwood, 166, 201; restoration, 166. *See also* Trees
Forster, E. M., *Passage to India*, 143–44
Free market, 114
French Cooking, 111–12
French Quarter, New Orleans, 110
Friendship, 122–26

Frogs, 67, 71–73; gray tree frog
    (*hyla versicolor*), 66–70
Fungi, 151–52

Gandhi, Mahatma, 13, 29
Ganesha, 39
Garden of Epicurus, 26–27, 113
Gardening, 49, 55, 61–62;
    composting, 59–61; drip
    watering, 53–54; earth worms,
    60–61; knapweed invasions,
    55–57; soil preparation, 49–50;
    the vegetable garden, 49–50,
    51–52, 57–59, 115
Gelbspan, Ross, *The Heat Is On*,
    203
Genetically modified foods, 84,
    120–21
Global warming, 28, 88, 159–61,
    173–74, 200, 203
Goodness, 28–29
Graveyard visit (autobiographical),
    99–100
Great Lakes, 87
Greenhouse effect, 28, 88, 159–61,
    173–74, 200, 203
Gregg Richard, "Voluntary
    Simplicity," 13

Hague conference, 159
Handwriting, 137
Hannum, Hunter and Hildegarde,
    143
Hardwood trees and forests, 166,
    201
"head labor," 138
Hearth (woodstove), 14–15, 155,
    158–59, 171
Herbicides, 84
Hillman, James, 10
Hinduism, 39, 72

Home and home furnishings (the
    author's), 9–10, 30–32, 33–35
Hopi kachinas, 37–38
Hospitality, 111, 112–13
Household economy, 12–13
Hughes, Langston, *First Book of
    Jazz*, 46–47
Hunter–gatherer ancestors, 193,
    194–95
Hunting technologies, 153–54

Impermanence, 16–17
Imprisoned man (autobiographical
    story), 64
India (trip to), 129
Individualism, 13
Industrial Revolution, 27
Industrial toxins, 192
Inequality, 15
Inland lakes, 87, 89; degradation
    of, 202–3; Great Lakes, 87;
    Lake Michigan, 201–2
Insect infestations, 150–51
Insects, 73–75, 75. *See also*
    Butterflies and caterpillars
    (*Lepidoptera*)
International Forum on
    Globalization, 190
International Union for the
    Conservation of Nature, 71
Interspecies violence, 91
Iron production, 158

Jains (Hindu), 72
Jazz, 46–47
Joyce, James, 1443

Kachina dolls, 37–38
Kali, 161–62
Keynes, John Maynard, 161
Kirkpatrick, Sale, 33

Knapweed, 55–57
Kwan Yin, 37
Kyoto conference, 150

Ladakh (trip to), 57
Lake Michigan, 201–2;
    degradation of, 202–3
Land developer (autobiographical
    story), 91–92
Land speculation, 92
Leopold, Aldo, 128–29, 166–67,
    196–97
Library (the author's), 141–45
Life, 66, 186–87; question of how
    to live, 27–28, 151, 168
Literacy, 127–29. *See also* Books
Literature and books, 141–45
Litter cleanup, 90
Lucretius, *The Nature of Things* (F.
    O. Copley, trans.), 21, 24,
    26–27, 175, 189–90
Luddites/Ludditism, 33, 134
Ludd, Neil, 33
Luke, Helen, 125
Lyons, Oren, 50, 191

McClure, Michael, 123
Maclean, Norman, *Young Men and
    Fire*, 162–63
MacLeish, William, *The Day
    Before America*, 65–66
Maple tree, 150, 166
Material simplicity, 3, 26, 189–91
Maul (wood-splitting tool),
    157–58
Metaphysics, 23
Metamorphosis: amphibian,
    70–71; in the order *Lepidoptera*,
    75, 77–79
Mexican cooking, 110
Midwest (upper), 4–5, 87; the

author's move to, 8–10, 11–12.
    See also Inland lakes; Seasons
Miles the bike mechanic (author's
    friend), 97–98
Milkweed, 76, 80
Mills, Stephanie, *In Service of the
    Wild*, 63
Mind–body dichotomy, 105–6
Misanthropy, 199
Mississippi (childhood visits to),
    110
Mochoacán mountains, 81
Monarch butterflies, 76, 77–79,
    84–85
Monarch butterfly reserves:
    Central Mexico (Sierra
    Chincua), 79, 81–83; Monterey
    Bay, 79
Monarch caterpillars, 76, 78, 80
Mookerjee, Ajit, *Kali*, 161–62
Mother Nature/Earth Mother,
    162, 206
Mourning process, 16–17, 187–88.
    See also Death
Muir, John, 65

Naess, Arne, 30. *See also* Deep
    ecology
Natural disasters, 160–61
Natural food coops, 115, 116–22;
    management issues, 119–20,
    121–22
Nature, 162, 199–200, 205–6;
    diminishing wilderness, 193;
    wilderness as healer, 64–65
Nearing, Helen and Scott, *Living
    the Good Life*, 138, 139
Needs, 1–3, 26
Nelson, Richard, 11
New Orleans, 110
Nietzsche, Friedrich, 175

Night sky, 11, 196
Nonprofit management, 119–20,
    121–22
Nonviolence, 72

Oak trees, 166
Oates, Whitney J., *The Stoic and
    Epicurean Philosophers,* 22, 24
O'Neill, Kathleen, 34
Organic farming, 107–8, 120. *See
    also* Food coops
Orion Society, 81, 82, 84
Orwell, George, "Why I Write,"
    129–30
Other(s), 63, 66, 91

Paganism, 199–200
Peshtigo fire, 163
Pesticides, 101–2
Phil (author's ex-husband), 8–9,
    51, 118, 176
Phoenix, childhood in, 6–7, 125,
    147–48
Place, sense of, 10–11
Pleasure, 25–26
Point Foundation, 112
Population growth, 50–51
Porcupine, 185–87
Primeval forest, 167
Primitive romanticism, 193
Progress, 12–13, 192, 204
Public speaking, 140
Pyne, Stephen J., 163

Ram Dass, 22
Random violence, 92–96
Reagan, Ronald, 204
Renewable energy, 155–56
Restoration, habitat, 63
Rio de Janeiro summit, 159
Ritual, 195, 197. *See also* Altar

Rob (author's friend), 10, 19
Rodents, voles, 179–80
Romanticism, primitive, 193
Rural development, residential,
    90–93
Rural living, 11–12, 15–16
Russell, Dick, 84
Ryan, John C., 98; and Alan Thein
    Durning, *Stuff,* 136

Sachs, Wolfgang, 190
Sand County farm, 166–67
San Francisco Bay Area, 5,
    113–14. *See also* Berkeley Co-
    op
Sauer, Peter, 82
Seasons: autumn, 147, 149–50,
    151, 152–53; spring, 41–42, 48;
    summer, 87–88, 103–4. *See also*
    Winter
Second-growth and later growth
    woodlots, 148–50
Seder, 112
Seed scattering, 152
Self-doubt, 124
Self-reliance, 115–16
Seneca, 21, 26
Senses and sensation, 21–22, 182
Sensuality of place, 10–11
Shepard, Paul, *The Tender Carnivore
    and the Sacred Game,* 55
Sierra Chincua monarch butterfly
    reserve, 79, 81–83
Simplicity: Epicurean, 2, 19,
    189–90; everyday living, 24,
    136; material simplicity, 3, 26,
    189–91; wants and needs, 1–3,
    26; Zen and, 154–55
Singer, Isaac Bashevis, 133
Skiing, cross-country, 176–77,
    184–85

Slippery Jacks, 151
Snow, 169–70, 171, 173, 174–76
Snyder, Gary, 191
Solitude, 13, 66, 132
Solstices: summer solstice, 103;
    winter solstice, 169–70
Sonoran Desert, 147–48
Soul, 182. *See also* Spirituality
Species extinctions, 200
Sphinx moth, 75
Spirituality, 42, 105; pagan,
    199–200; the soul, 182
Spring, 41–42, 48
Squash, 62
Suburban sprawl, 92, 148
Sugar maple, 150, 166
Summer, 87–88, 103–4; summer
    solstice, 103
Supermarkets/chain-stores,
    120–21
Swimming, 88–90, 92–93

Taboos, 197–99
Tamarack City, 8, 30
Television, 32–33
Thanatos and Eros, 204
Thoreau, Henry David, 1, 64, 157
Tolstoy, Leo, 13
Tomato hornworm, 75–76
Tom (author's friend), 52–53
Toxic pollution, 192
Tree-cutting, 149, 156, 158; clear-
    cutting, 166; maximum harvest,
    166; to reduce fire hazard,
    164–66
Tree planting, 166
Trees, 148–49; beech, 150, 160,
    166; first growth, 167;
    hardwood, 166, 201; maple,
    150, 166; oak, 166
Typewriters, 134–35

United Nations Conference on
    Environment and Development,
    159

Vegetable garden, 49–50, 51–52,
    57–59, 115
Violence: intraspecies, 91; random,
    92–96
Vocation, 127, 131, 139. *See also*
    Writing
Voles, 179–80

Wallace, William, 22, 23, 26–27
Wants and needs, 1–3, 26
Water carrying, 54
Watering, drip, 53–54
Water quality, 95
Waters, Frank, *Book of the Hopi*,
    38
Wedding (autobiographical), 9
West, Rebecca, *Black Lamb and
    Grey Falcon*, 128
Whaleback Bay beach, 201–2
Whitman, Walt, 179
Wilde, Oscar, 83, 105
Wilderness: diminishing, 193; as
    healer, 64–65
Wildfire, 162–64
Wildlife, 11, 42–43; habitats,
    63–64, 179
Wild, living in the, 193–97
Windmills, 155–56
Winter, 19–20, 31, 169, 177–78;
    coldness, 170–71; cross-country
    skiing, 176–77, 184–85; snow,
    169–70, 171, 173, 174–76;
    winter garments, 172–73;
    winter solstice, 169–70
Wood: firewood, 157; wood
    splitting, 156, 157–58. *See also*
    Tree-cutting

Woodstove, 14–15, 155, 158–59,
171
Word-processing, 135
World Conservation Union, 71
World market, 82
Writing, 44, 129–34, 138;
deadlines, 132–33; as a
livelihood, 139–40; not writing,
132–34; as sedentary work,
133, 170; tools of, 134–37; as a
vocation, 127, 131, 139

Writing studio (the author's),
35–36, 141

Zen teachings and simplicity,
154–55
Zitácuaro, 81. *See also* Sierra
Chincua monarch butterfly
reserve